The Secrets of the Sacred Cat of Burma

The Secrets of the Sacred Cat of Burma

BIRMAN HISTORY

English Edition by
ALWYN HILL

Original Authors

SIMONE POIRIER &
GISÈLE BARNAY

LitPrime
"Your story is our priority"

LitPrime Solutions
21250 Hawthorne Blvd
Suite 500, Torrance, CA 90503
www.litprime.com
Phone: 1-800-981-9893

Published by LitPrime Solutions   01/30/2023

ISBN: 979-8-88703-142-2(sc)
ISBN: 979-8-88703-143-9(hc)
ISBN: 979-8-88703-144-6(e)

Library of Congress Control Number: 2023900023

CONTENTS

Pat Beck painted this beautiful picture in 1980

PREFACE TO THE ENGLISH EDITION

· · · · · · ● ● ● ● ● ● · · · ·   · · · · ● ● ● ● ● ● ● · · · ·

had always wanted to know exactly what was said during that conversation between Simone Poirier and Gisele Barnay. The story of the Birman is so fascinating I wanted to share it with others so I set out on a journey to find the owner of the book and ask them to please print this English version or allow me to have an English reprint produced. In the process I was lucky to find Arlette Poirier, Simone's daughter and I was fortunate that she helped me in my quest. I would also like to thank others who have given their time and effort too:

Julie Collin President of the Sacred Cat of Burma Fanciers in America for allowing me to use photographs from the Club archives. Linda and Mevin Gregory, Betty Brown, Joyce Worth, Mathilde Bonetti, Roberta Bianchi, Claire Anne Fraii, Vivian Creasey-Smith author of 'The Birman Cat World Wide'. Also all those friends round the world, who have encouraged me to pursue the ambition to see this English Edition in print.

A special big thank you to: Michelle and her husband Clive for all their hard work translating the book.

I have selected a slightly different lay out for this book but where changes have taken place there are notes. I have also taken the advantage of inserting pictures of as many named cats as I could find many of which did not appear in the original book.

Alwyn Hill

PREFACE

The Idea had been in the air for many years. There are those sentences, dropped casually into conversation, which one forgets and which come up again another day, one doesn't know how. Without you knowing it, the idea has matured and demands attention. Those little words "How about we write a book together?" were said. When? We've forgotten. It was a very long time ago.

I met Simone Poirier for the first time in 1972. She was one of those great ladies of the feline fancy. She was a specialist in Birman cats and assistant to Marguerite Ravel, the General Secretary of the Paris Cat Club since 1934. I was the Chief Editor of *La Vie des Betes* (The Life of Animals) and in order to do a good job, it was necessary to speak to the best person. I was therefore naturally pointed in the direction of Simone Poirier-who had already written in the magazine herself-for my first "paper" on The Sacred Cat of Burma. A magazine article, even a specialised one, is not able to say everything. It had to be deleted, shortened, condensed: in brief, left wanting more. It was perhaps during this period or a little later that one of us said for the first time those famous little words, which were to launch us on the Birman trail.

Fifteen years have passed and the book is here at last! God knows we have faced problems: being given a lead only to then take a backward step, because the first breeders of Birman cats worked jealously to guard their secrets of selection in the same way that a great chef, who is cautious, does not hand out his recipes. The essence, the knack and that little *extra* which makes their dish matchless, is their secret, their creation and so in certain situations, we had to put forward the most plausible hypotheses, based on one or other of the authentic documents from the Twenties and Thirties. The eyes of the Birman-blue like azure stone, the lapis-lazuli, the silky coat of the Birman-sheer poetry, the white gloves of the Birman-a distinctly important mark, which made him from the beginning a little god, destined to be a legend.

The first breeders had imagination and as Marcel Adams would have said, "a pretty bit of fluff." Their Birman cats deserve this lyricism: there was no question of forgetting them in this book. Moreover, there are comments made by a Birman specialist, a zoologist and a geneticist.

The second and third chapters are of great importance. Simone Poirier, either more generous or more modern than her predecessors, confides her secrets of selection, because she has loved and bred this superb cat too long to suffer the stupid things said about and done to the breed. She says "I think that what I have achieved with the breed has been destroyed over the last few years" We go back to the post-war years, when Simone Poirier became, in her turn, fascinated by the Birman cat, and decided to return it to its past glory. The breeding cats of her "stable" were the descendants of three well-known Birmans Orloff: born in 1943 and his daughters Xenia and Xanthippe de Kaabaa and they came from prestigious lines: Kaabaa from Mlle Boyer and Madalpour, from Mme Chaumont-Doisy, who had recovered the original suffix of the Birman cat.

I asked questions tirelessly, Simone Poirier replied patiently and sometimes she said, "You remind me of inspector Colombo!" Simone has so many stories that I found it was not possible to leave anything uncovered. I was merciless besides, the passion for this cat is infectious: Onyx, a blue Birman, has shared my life for the last twelve years…I have had time to observe him, but my observations have been on a single subject, but no one bothers with the observations of breeders. Which brings us completely naturally to speak about genetics; this is an era that cannot ignore the monumental discovery of the botanist Gregor Mendal. There will be no scientific discussion in this book, which is aimed at all Birman cat-lovers. There will only be a short account of the difficulties with their breeding, so you will love them more.

Their pretty white gloves, which give them the

elegance of a ballet dancer, what a problem they are! They must maintain the standard of mittens or slippers, never to become "long gloves" or "socks" above all they must not disappear! And so I thought, when cuddling Onyx, Vichnou or Poupee, about the concerns of the breeder at the birth of a kitten: "has he or has he not got good regular gloves?" Because the kittens are born white, one must wait many days and have a perfectly trained eye to detect the gloves on a scarcely coloured paw.

In short, every cat with a superb cream ruff, masked in seal or blue and gloved in white, possesses a genotype inherited from its ancestors. The genotype cannot be forced when introducing another breed, which will bring with it a multicoloured wardrobe. "Be careful" said Simone Poirier, "the creation of new strains, with different colourings, demands a strict breeding program to ensure that the breed is not damaged." On this score she agrees with Marcel Baudoin-Crevoisier, one of the first Birman breeders, the "creator of the famous Dieu D'Arakan who was already concerned in 1967 about the vogue in the blue Birman. He had said: "The Birman cat is an animal of an almost supernatural beauty. It is a crime of treason to want to change those characteristics!" What would he have said when faced with the latest creations, red and tortoiseshell Birmans recognised by the International Cat Federation?

A French cat, the seal Birman wants to maintain its "French Quality" and yet the same cat carries the English title "seal point" on its identity card-sorry, its standard-for many years. Today it has made small inroads into all the countries of the world. Each country has its own group protecting the breed, including the United States, where it arrived in 1959. Great Britain followed suit in 1965. Belgium, Switzerland and Italy have adopted and loved this cat since the beginning of the Thirties. It has conquered Europe-Germany, Austria, Holland, Luxembourg, the Scandinavian countries etc. and also Canada, Latin America, Australia and Japan… The breed originated in Asia. Here or there, in the ancient or New World the Birman cat cares not. Dignified, handsome, he holds the look of Poupee de Madalpour, his ancestor, in his fur, whether light or bronzed; he understands all languages; he lets himself be admired and he loves all who love him. No one is insensible to his charm. Simone Poirier said, "Today I received some more letters from people who bought cats from me ten, fifteen, or more, years ago. They send me photos, they tell me about the death of a wonderful Birman who was part of the family.

Birman cat lovers are inexhaustible; they must be allowed to speak. We have found in the personal diaries of Madeleine Boyer, the story of Fly de Kaabaa, the grandfather of Orloff, most of today's Birmans, are his descendants it is a touching document and unpublished. Unshakeably thoroughbred but playful and cuddly, the Birman tiptoes through the fifth chapter. In passing he comes within a whisker of and seduces a young female, a grand actress who we loved very much, a "cat" herself: Romy Schneider. It is the story of Balzac, the secret life of a splendid seal point, intertwines with the life of

Romy, which was interrupted too early. There is also the story of Jessy, a kitten who fell from the second floor and was seriously injured. She was nursed so well that she became an international champion, faithful all her life…to a common tomcat. Whether moving or amusing, these anecdotes prove that the Birman is full of things to say, just as is Simone Poirier, in whose home so many "sacred cats" have been born.

The last cat adored by Simone was Semele de Mun Ha, who died in 1986 at the age of seventeen. We find her again with Poupee and Manou de Madalpour, Dieu d'Arakan, Cosima des Muses, Fantine, Namour and Marquis de Crespiere, Ophelie and Olympio, Princesse de Ranchipur, Wladimir de Pouh Milo, Ines de Pagan and others, throughout this book, which is dedicated to them.

Gisele Barnay

CHAPTER 1

THE MYSTERY OF THE ORIGIN

Gisele Barnay.   When did you first hear about the Birman cat?

Simone Poirier.   That is a tale in itself. I lost my husband in February 1952. My daughter and I were feeling very alone, and wanted to have a cat, but the breed of cat was very important: a Siamese. I didn't know where to find one and at the beginning of the summer I was taking a stroll along the banks of the Seine. There are shops selling animals on the embankment, and I saw some poor sad little cats but no Siamese. I returned home. I was living at that time in the seventeenth district of Paris, in "Rue Saint-Ferdinand" Whilst walking along "Rue des Acacias," I went into a dog grooming parlour. I asked the owner if, amongst her clients, she had heard of a breeder of Siamese cats. She replied "you should buy a Birman cat. I have seen some at the Cat Club Show-they are superb!" and she gave me the address of the Countess of Maubou, who had left her with her card.

GB.   Who was the Countess of Maubou?

SP.   She was an actress of the Twenties, Yahne Lambray, who had married the Count of Maubou. One day I went to her house, in "Rue de Rivoli." I saw three beautiful cats with mid length coats, cream with brown marking like the Siamese, they had little white "slippers" on their paws: one male, Agni and two females, Aicha and Addy de Kaabaa. There were many more kittens all seal pointed. The Countess of Maubou had bought them from Mlle Boyer, one of the first Birman breeders. These three cats were the offspring of Xenia and Orloff de Kaabaa, the two descendants from the first Birmans. Orloff survived until the war in 1940.

GB.   Was it love at first sight?

SP.   Not at all! When I saw the way the Birman cat looked, so profound, with eyes so blue, I was fascinated. However when the Countess told me that a female cost 18,000 francs, I realised their great weakness!

GB.   18,000 francs in 1952 that was a lot! And so?

SP.   I was not able to pay that amount. For 6,000 francs Countess of Maubou offered me Yago, a big neutered Siamese who was without a pedigree and Brinbelle; she was a little hybrid female cat. Brinbelle was the daughter of Yago and a seal point Siamese. She had a mid length coat and was very cute: she had a round head and dark blue round eyes: her fur was very light beige, with brown markings. She had a little of Yago's look about her. The male, a typical Siamese, had a very short smooth coat, where as Brinbelle was a little "angora" but without the white gloves of the Birman breed.

Left to Right: Siddharto, Prince de Birmanie, Yago, Yagoll and Lemirvano Owned by M Dugum

GB. Has the Siamese cat got a round head?

SP. Yes, and the same dark blue, round eyes. Yago was like a force of nature, he was big, full of life and he kept clambering about all the time. He was a little exhausting! In 1952, the Siamese cat was not a fragile creature. In any case, I did not want to keep a crossbred cat.

GB. Were you happy with your Siamese cats?

SP. Yes, very much so. I found them so very restless but they got on well and they played together. Brinbelle was almost six months old: she was born on 22 June 1952. She was grown up but at that time I had not thought about choosing a stud. Countess of Maubou encouraged me to mate Brinbelle to Agni, her male Birman.

GB. What was he like?

SP. He had a little of the morphology of the Siamese of the time, a little heavier, with strong paws: all four paws had white gloves, but not perfect ones. His eyes were very blue. I finally decided on the union! Agni produced only one kitten by Brinbelle: a female who proved to be superb, in accordance with the standards of the day. She had a beautiful silky coat, a very bushy ruff and sapphire blue eyes. She did not however have any gloves so later I gave her to a friend who had her spayed.

GB. Were you disappointed?

SP. Yes a little. I had to keep Brinbelle indoors in order to breed from her. I thought about beginning breeding Birmans a year later.

GB. It was then 1953. Were you interested in cat shows?

SP. Not really. I was not ready, my Siamese cats were registered with the Cat Club but I had not placed them in any cat shows. I did not go to them; I had my cats for company.

GB. Did you remain in contact with the Countess of Maubou?

SP. Yes, she often invited me to tea, and she would talk to me about poems she had written. We would talk about everything, mostly poetry and art, not always about cats. She certainly had an idea at the back of her mind regarding selling me a Birman cat but she was patient, she let me "Ripen" At that time it was the summer of 1953. I had resisted the temptation for a long time, but not for much longer.

GB. Did Countess of Maubou know the origins of the Birman? Was she concerned about it?

SP. I don't know. She was more lyrical than technical. She spoke to me above all about the famous legend of the Birman cat, which has been peddled and well known since 1926. This legend, that tells how the first Birman cats had gathered in a temple in Northern Burma, before the First World War, has something interesting about it. I was not very gullible, but it "gelled" perfectly with the manner of the Birman cat. I had to have something to dream about and I did not ask any more questions. Much later I asked myself many questions, but I could not always find the answers.

GB. It's true from its appearance in cat shows that

this cat has always been shown in a romantic way. I was astonished to discover the beginnings of the legend in a thesis for a veterinary doctorate: the thesis on breeds of cats submitted by Philippe Jumaud at the faculty of medicine in Lyon on 25th March 1925. In it he presents, amongst other breeds the cat of Burma: like the Siamese this cat is from the Far East. The Birman cats, bred in temples, were very heavily guarded and their removal was forbidden. Nevertheless, some years ago M. Vanderbilt thought he would acquire a pair, whose offspring have provided the basis of our observations. In an article in *Vie a la Campagne* "Country Life" in October 1926, Doctor Jamaud wrote that the pair had been imported by Mme Thadde-Hadish. (*The documents are printed at the end of this chapter*) In another later article published in December 1925, he quotes "the most Rare Birman cats" without other comment.

SP. It is probably because the story was so muddled and mysterious that I did not dig any deeper. In any case the story which Countess of Maubou told was the same one as told in books and many other magazine articles. If my memory serves me well Doctor Jamaud published a book in 1926-7. There was another by a Swiss Abbot, Marcel Reney, in 1947 and the articles of Baudoin-Crevoisier, on the Birman breeders at the end of the Twenties, carried the same opinion: I found these later magazines dated from before the war.

GB. The breeders kept the mystery alive. I have read

it all, and it is like a detective novel, or adventure story. It all started in the mythical temple of Lao-tsun with Sir Russell Gordon, a foreign major from the Indian army, Augustus Pavie, a true French diplomat, M Vanderbilt, an American multimillionaire, and two high flying adventurers: Mme Thadde-Hadish, from Vienna and Mme Leotardi, apparently from Nice. (*All these people were listed in the work by Marcel Reney,* Nos amis les chats *Published by Ch Grasset in Geneva 1947) Also see in the documents at the end of this chapter, an extract from article by Philippe Jumaud in 1926.*

Left to Right Sin, Lon Golden, Sita I, Nafaghi de Madalpour and Champion Poupee De Madalpour

According to Marcel Baudoin-Crevoisier, Poupee, the grandmother of all our Birmans, was born in Nice.

SP.   There at least is a certainty; the Birman cat was bred in the Midi area of France around 1923-24.

GB. That corresponds perfectly with the thesis written by Philippe Jumaud, the vet at Saint Raphael. He wrote in March 1925: "The breeding of the subjects has been particularly difficult. He confirms this difficulty in his article of October 1926. Mme Leotardi, who has had the opportunity to breed more litters, confirms that one should reckon to breed no more than one good one in ten.

SP. They all admit that the breeding of Birman Cats was, from the beginning, shrouded in mystery and a lot of hypothesising has been done. For example, the breeder or breeders may have used a hybrid, a white-gloved Siamese stud, with a queen with long hair. Or a hybrid "angora" Siamese stud with a queen with little white gloves. They kept one cat in ten from their crosses, the one who had Siamese markings, the longer coat and had little gloves.

GB. Perhaps the very first cross was not planned? I read in the July 1927 issue of *Vie a La Campagne* a severe warning aimed at cat breeders in general: You must make allowances, with only rare exceptions, for all the mismatches which result from accidental liaisons.

Champion Poupee de Madalpour Owner Mme Leotardi

SP.   If it was an accident, the mysterious Mme Leotardi had a good idea about accidental selection! In any case our hypotheses are plausible: There were Siamese and Persians in France in the Twenties. Anyway, the first valuable result was the famous Poupee de Madalpour, the star of the cat show in Paris in 1926. Poupee passed her gloves to many of her descendants. The kittens were kept which had the best-defined gloves, important, as this characteristic is passed on from generation to generation. So the breed came into existence and the Madalpour stock came to show it off.

GB.   Yes! The appearance of Poupee was well orchestrated. She was given good press as they say today.

SP.   Dr Jumaud was the general secretary of the first French cat club, the Cat Club of France and Belgium; it was founded in 1913. It was he who organised the first show, before the 1914 war.

GB.   According to the magazines of the twenties, they had cat shows in provincial locations: in Nice and Cannes from 1912 and in Aix-les-Bains in 1914. They were gradually reintroduced after the war, notably in Cannes in 1923. The great international cat show of Paris in 1926 was the first of its kind. In the history of breeding pedigree, cats it was the date which counted.

SP.   I believe that it was planned for January 1926 but they had many problems.

GB.   The show had to be cancelled in January, due to the cold and the difficulty of keeping the cats warm enough, it was finally held on 14th and 15th May. Approximately three hundred cats were shown, mainly very beautiful Persians and Siamese. Jacques Nam designed the cover of the catalogue; he was a painter and poet of cats at the time.

SP.   The Birman cat was an event at that show.

GB.   I have found some interesting reviews: "We noticed with great pleasure the interest taken in the Persian cat. The cat of Burma, so rare, that those admired by the public at Paris are perhaps the only known living examples of the breed" Only three Birmans were shown but the well-known Poupee was the most remarked-upon. Another comment was: "good examples of this breed are rare, but those shown were very attractive, in particular Poupee de Madalpour owned by Mme Leotardi presents all the characteristics of the breed."

SP. She has already had her story told by Marcelle Adam, who was extremely interested in the Birman cat.

GB. The veterinary doctor Fernand Mery had published that story in1925 in Minerva, a weekly publication, from before the war, to which he contributed. He wrote in an article of 1926 the story told to him "by a friend of animals and poets" Thirty years later, in his work Sa Majeste le Chat (His Majesty the Cat), he named his blonde friend: Mme Marcelle Adam.

SP. Marcelle Adam was a novelist of the twenties, a contemporary of Collette. She had written Moune, Femme d'artiste (Moune, the Artist's Woman) but her name was mainly linked with the promotion of the Birman cat. At the cat show the following year she showed a superb male Birman who belonged to her: Manou de Madalpour.

GB. There was a passion for 'jumping on the band wagon' back then! Cat shows multiplied in 1927: at Bordeaux, Strasbourg, Charleville. The second great international show of the Cat Club of France and Belgium was held in Paris on the 14th and 15th January 1927. The reviews of the show, on the subject of the Birman, were brief and did not do them justice. Two lines in *Vie a la Campagne:* "Three beautiful Birman cats, already shown in 1926, had fur that might be described as mid-length" Not a word about Birmans in *Chasse Peche Elevage* (Hunting, Fishing Breeding) although mention was made of "a couple of pink cats from Turkey, with short hair, of light beige with a red sheen."

SP. There was another international cat show in May 1927, organised by the Central Feline Society of France, founded the previous year. The General Secretary was M Guingand.

Marcelle Adam holding Manou de Madalpour

GB. Indeed. Moreover, Dr Mery had participated in the organisation of this show. Manou de Madalpour made an appearance and one is able to read in Minerva that he had won first prize.

In another magazine, one comes across Collette: She had shown two Chartreux cats, called at that time Auvergne cats or American cats! Three hundred cats of all colours, coats and varieties occupied their little cages, which were prettily decorated according to the whim of their owners. Here, a little Chinese temple, behind which, next to an incense stick and a little bronze Buddha sat the admirable Birman cat of Mme Marcelle Adam. There, in a corner covered in satin Mme Collette jealously showed her two smoke-grey American cats, which she did not have patience to keep imprisoned until the end of the event.

SP.   I remember well that Manou de Madalpour was the only Birman cat present at the Central Feline Society Show with permission of the Cat Club of Paris, part of the Cat club of France. The breed was not easy one to create.

GB.   A single Birman competed, effectively, at this show. There were comments in the papers of the time: "It is unfortunate that this pretty breed has not expanded further. However it did not exist until a few years ago in France. The Birman coat and his qualities have to be the same as the Siamese: light colour coat, a distinctive mask of otter-brown and with beautiful blue eyes, but where the Siamese have short fur, that of the Birman is long and their four paws are gloved in white.

SP.   The breeders had settled upon the characteristics "long-haired" fairly easily and also the Siamese markings but the gloves posed them a large number of problems.

GB. At the fourth international cat show in Paris, run by the Central Feline Society and the Cat Club of Paris, on the 4th and 5th May 1928 and organised by Salle Wagram, there were no more than seven or eight Birman cats, all from de Madalpour stock. There were write-ups and photographs of Poupee, the champion owned by Mme Leotardi, and Nafaghi, owned by M and Mme Gilbert. The male cats Manou, owned by Mme Marcelle Adam and Hiram-Roi. Their prizes were said to be 7 to 10.000 francs for the best cats, Poupee and Manou and 3 to 4.000 francs for the not so beautiful cats.

SP. It was said that the less beautiful ones had a little more of the Siamese morphology and irregular gloves. It was also said that the look of the Birman was difficult to achieve and was at risk of becoming extinct. Yet breeders had begun to take an interest in this breed. Marcel Baudoin appeared on the scene. He gave a series of lectures about breeding Birmans. His cats were successful.

GB. It is undeniable. Articles of the thirties did not shed any light on the mystery of their origins! The origin of the Birman cat was very controversial: many people asserted that it was achieved by crossing a Siamese with a white Persian.

SP. Yes they did say that, for sure. Philippe Jumaud claimed that Siamese and Persian cats refused to mate!

He wrote as much in 1926. The Birman cat had come from the Far East and he was immovable on that point.

GB. Nowhere is it said that somewhere on the coast of Singapore, a street cat with Siamese markings did not mate with a longhaired cat but on the other hand nothing has come along to prove that Birman breeding happened in the Far East.

SP. When I was doing my breeding, I did a fair amount of research. I often tried to obtain information by writing letters but mostly by asking questions of people, mainly those who had been to Burma. They always replied that they had never come across cats with long hair, in the Far East, who looked like our Birman cats. One day, I hope but we will come back to that: it was a false road.

GB. No one has ever seen a Birman in Burma: there is no mention of the cat in the mythology or folklore of Burma. For zoologists, the trail leads towards a wild cat of the Far East.

Professor Paul Schauenberg, attached to the research department at the Museum of Geneva, studied the cat very closely. On the subject of the Siamese, he said conditionally: "The cat of Bengal *prionailurus bengalensis*, the most common cat breed in Asia would become-for various authors-responsible for certain characteristics peculiar to the Siamese cat and some other emerging breeds." Professor Bernard Conde, a researcher at the Zoological Museum at Nancy, cited in my first book about these cats: *Les Plus Beaux Chats de France* (The Most Beautiful Cats In France) and two ancient naturalists Pousargues and Gyldenstolpe, who supported this thesis after they had visited south-east Asia in the Nineteenth Century.

I also consulted Professor Dreux, who was a lecturer at the University of Pierre and Marie Curie in Paris. "There exists in the world" he said "a great number of breeds of little wild cats, and just about all of them are able to breed amongst themselves whilst in captivity and also, in the same circumstances, with local domesticated cats, which produced different hybrids.

The domestication of the cat is another story and a very complex one, "it appears that there are two main areas where domestication occurred: one in Egypt, which has been more greatly studied, and the other in the Far East, for which there is very little knowledge." Did the Siamese derive itself from the Bengal cat, crossed with another wild Asian breed, like the cat of the steppes of Asia (*Felis s.ornata*)? "It is possible. The Siamese has a voice completely different to that of other cats. There is often a behavioural difference between the Siamese and other breeds of cat."

Finally was the Siamese cat bred in Asia? "It is plausible," said Professor Dreux, "but it is difficult to know in which era. I am almost convinced, in the case, that the Siamese cat differentiated itself from the other breeds of cats."

SP. It would be interesting to know if the first Birmans had the voice of the Siamese. I have never read about that anywhere. Marcel Baudoin wrote that Poupee de Madalpour had been mated to a Siamese with very blue eyes accordingly named "the cat of Laos" belonging to a doctor in Nice. Then, by successive crosses (but he does not say with what breed), the breeders were finally able to obtain a cat as beautiful as its mother Poupee: the famous Manou of Mme Marcelle Adam. In 1926-27 Poupee gave birth to other kittens with fairly good gloves: the male kittens Sinh and Lon Golden and the females Sita II (named after Poupee's mother Sita) and Nafaghi amongst others.

GB. If one continues the tour of the cat shows of the era, one sees the arrival of other stars. There were two more "show" cats in 1929 in Paris: one at the Cat Club show on the 8th - 9th February and the other at the Central Feline Society show on 24th -26th May. They were a couple of Birman cats unique in the world on account of their perfection." This referred to Ijadi Tsun, a female cat and the male Lon Saito born in 1927, when Marcel Baudoin became their owner.

SP. 1929 was the year when Baudoin began to work seriously on the breed. He never made any secret of avoiding "too many incestuous unions" he made " lucky out-crosses with some Siamese females with white gloves and some stud-cats of Madalpour's line" but never admitted that he had called in some Persians.

GB. Upon seeing the results in the following years, it is undeniable! In the photos, the cats of Marcel Baudoin-Crevoisier have a head distinctly more rounded and fur much longer than found with other breeders. Have you never had the chance to meet him and ask that question?

SP. I met Marcel Baudoin-Crevoisier many years later, in 1967 I believe. A breeder I did not know brought me a queen for mating. It was she who brought me in contact with Baudoin. He had not had any Birman cats for almost thirty-five years. When I asked him the question: "What did you use for your breeding?" he replied "a Siamese, gloved and with long fur."

GB. He surely would have wanted to speak of Sita, the mother of Poupee de Madalpour, since he had, as you might say, jumped onto a moving train.

SP. Probably, in any case, he responded to all my explicit questions in an evasive manner, clouding the trail. He was bizarre; he stuck to the history, always gliding over any doubts of their origin. I could not get any clear answers. He waited for me to give him news of his cats, long since dead but I had no idea what had become of them.

GB. According to the chronicles of the Thirties, he did not breed Birmans for very long: only between 1929 and 1933. He must have become quickly discouraged.

SP. He had found it was too difficult, when perhaps the breeding did not bring him the luck that he had hoped for. It may have been he who produced the most beautiful subjects of the pre war period, but he lacked perseverance, which was a shame.

GB. Yes, it is a shame. His greatest success, his marvel Dieu d'Arakan, was born in 1930, and presented in the class of young males on the 11th and 12th April 1931 at the second international cat show in Reims, organised by the Cat Club of Champagne, where he carried of his first prize.

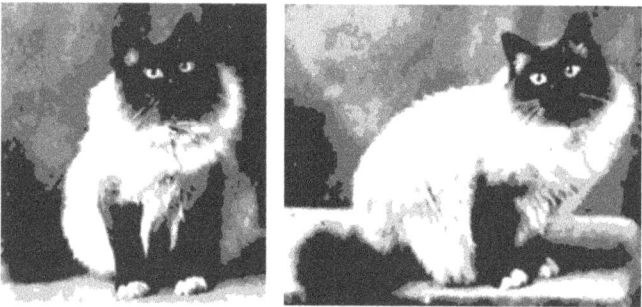

The famous Eu Ch Dieu d'Arakan in 1931:
from the side and front to show off his amazing ruff.
He was the most beautiful Birman cat of the Thirties.

In the "female open" class, Reine de Rangoon won a

first prize, she too was bred by Baudoin. The press was enthusiastic: "we have remarked on the splendid Birman cats Reine de Rangoon and Dieu d'Arakan.

At the seventh international show of the Cat Club of Paris, it was Djaipour, a male brought by Mme de Marigny, who won the first prize in the "kitten class." The show took place in January and Dieu d'Arakan was without doubt too young to take part.

SP.   There is no doubt that Baudoin had done a good job, with an intelligent breeding program that he continued to use. The original Madalpour line from which his stud Lon Saito came was good. The descendants of Poupee had been produced using regular blood relations with the intervention of Siamese cats, certainly gloved and probably with long coats. It was a prudent and controlled intervention, since the gloves were inherited by the new generations. Baudoin continued to "frequently renew the blood of the breeding cats" He wrote that but he certainly did not tell how!

GB.   It is true that in some specialised papers he gave some advice about prudent breeding. He wrote that breeding the choice of subjects is not easy (one suspected as much) "the male should be, at the very least, perfect, even if the female is not. Within this way of thinking, you would do well to cross a male Birman with a female Siamese with white gloves."

SP. It is necessary to specify that the Siamese was much less long limbed than today and that white markings on the paws were fairly frequent at that time, within the Siamese breed. That which was a disqualifying defect in one house became a quality sought after in another.

GB. Baudoin also specified that the Siamese and the Birman cats share their origins and he added "a crossed Birman and a gloved Siamese produced, in the second generation, a strong proportion of Birman characteristics. And these cats, from new crosses between themselves, produced kittens with at least 80-90% Birman characteristics." Perhaps he was lucky.

SP. It is possible. We will come back to that in the chapter on genetics! It is always possible for Baudoin to be judged by his results. In the cat shows of 1932, the cats of Marcel Baudoin-Crevoisier took away all the prizes.

GB. I checked all this in the papers for that year! At the Cat Club of Paris show in January and the Cat Club of Champagne show at Reims in February, they were all ecstatic! "The Birman cats were splendid, the international champions Dieu dArakan, Lon Saito de Madalpour and the amusing Reine de Rangoon, all from M Baudoin."

The second prize went to Zaquelle de Mandalay, also

from Baudoin's breeding and owned by Mlle Rouselle. For him 1932 was a glorious year. Birman cats were even celebrated in the columns of a specialist magazine, the *Kathimerini* in Athens.

SP. Dieu d'Arakan was superb. He showed off some magnificent eyes, which the black and white photos do not even give an inkling of. The quality of his fur was perfect and quite close to the actual standard. He was more squat, and more round headed than the first Birman cats, as you have already remarked.

GB. Did the success of Marcel Baudoin cause disruption to some vocations?

SP. It was inevitable. Many more breeders of the Siamese, including Mme Chaumont-Doisy, became interested in the Birman cat from the beginning of the 1930, but they succeeded with more or less good luck. Mlle Boyer also began at this time and she did some good work.

GB. I have noticed, in the photos of the thirties, that all the Birmans pictured did not necessarily have gloves. It was in certain situations difficult, to differentiate them from the Siamese who were a little round.

*Hueldeda de Madalpour a pretty female Birman
owned by Mme Chaumont-Doisy*

SP. It was probably the result of excessive crosses with the Persian. It is difficult to put a finger on it. When one loses gloves through some ill-considered cross, it takes five generations to find them again.

GB. The French didn't lose everything for all that, since they bred the Khmer from the Persian and Siamese. I have seen some very pretty photos of Khmers owned by M. Rieger, who also had some Siamese cats, in the papers of 1934.

SP. France soon gave up breeding the Khmer, who was called "the poor man's Birman" and finally adopted the Persian colour point bred in Great Britain before the war. Meanwhile, the breeding of the Birman cat continued.

Prince Roi Pi-You
a Khmer who won 1ˢᵗ prize at the
Paris cat show in 1934

GB. You can find in specialised magazines, in places of honour, the names of cats bred by Baudoin: Soleil d'Arakan, Bouli d'Arakan, Roult d'Arakan, Prince de Rangoon and of course Dieu d'Arakan, the beautiful males! Also the females Rose de Magock, Poupee de Rangoon, her daughter, Reine de Rangoon and Zaquelle de Mandalay. I am astonished that Marcel Baudoin did not have a suffix for his cattery.

SP. At the time that he began his breeding, they did not register suffices. The usage of suffices became common a little later.

GB. Probably at the same time as the Cat Club and the Central Feline Society were set up. The press announced the split between the Cat club of Paris, whose secretary was Mlle Tzaut, and the Cat Club of

France, of Philippe Jumaud, in November 1931. Some suffices were registered from 1932.

SP. It was recognised that suffices greatly simplified matters. Now, when I hear a suffix, I immediately know the name of the breeder.

GB. In fact, whilst French cat breeding improved and gained structure, Marcel Baudoin became discouraged! In June 1932 he wrote that his financial affairs were difficult and that cat food was expensive, etc.

SB. I do not know the motive for his behaviour but he did indeed sell the whole of his breeding stock in 1933.

GB. In an article published 1933, The Abbot Marcel Chamonin, a Swiss breeder of Siamese cats, confirmed Marcel Baudoun's withdrawal. He quoted a text published in *Revue Feline de France* (Cat Magazine of France) in July of the same year "and as for Birmans, alas, the breed cannot win. The great effort that we have personally made has not been continued, and yet we live in hope…"

SP. I certainly know that article by Abbot Chamonin. He sent out an alarm cry in the same way: "The Birman cat is in danger! Because of inbreeding, the females are now fragile and the males are mediocre reproducers." He proposed energetic intervention, the creation of the International Birman Cat Club, the betterment of the breed by the verification of pedigrees, strict observation of hereditary laws and the creation of an up-to-date book of origins etc.

GB.   The Birman cat was his passion. Abbot Chamonin had bought two from Baudoin: Rose de Mogock, the daughter of Bijou de Madalpour and an unknown mother and Poupee de Rangoon, born on 30th December, the daughter of Rose de Magock and Mouki an unknown Birman or Persian. Marcel Chamonin would regularly publish the results created by his two pretty females and his stud Fakir de la Chesnaie (*Chesnaie was Abbot Chamonin's Suffix*) Fakir was well gloved on all four paws, and came to him from another French breeder. Two other champions bred by Marcel Baudoin were sold, in Belgium, to Mlle Rousselle, the general secretary of the Cat Club of Liege. They were Lon Saito de Madalpour, born in 1927 and Zaquelle de Mandalay, born in 1931. Finally, his two wonders Dieu dArakan and Rene de Rangoon left together to live in Italy.

SP.   When I met Marcel Baudoin-Crevoisier in 1967, he first of all asked me if I was able to tell what had happened to his two most beautiful cats, sold to an Italian princess. I did not have any news about them. I only knew the book written by Marcel Reney published in 1947. In the book he said that he went to the Francecavilla-Bisio castle, near Novi-Ligure, in 1936. There he saw Dieu d'Arakan and Reine de Rangoon, surrounded by seventeen cats and their fourteen kittens. Since then, no one has heard any more about them.

GB. The only other person to see those cats was Marcel Reney, if we can believe his account. He was also the only person to tell of their astonishing adventure. Baudoin had sold his cats to Princess Ratibor Hohenlohe in 1933, for the sum of 30,000 francs. She had given them to the Duke of Aoste. They had finally landed up at the Francavilla-Bisio castle, the home of a cousin of the Duke of Aoste, the Countess Elisabetta Giriodi-Panissero, who seemed to love the animals a great deal. When she died in January 1985, she did not own a single cat, but she always had about thirty dogs. Mme Norma Bagnasco, still responsible for the bursar's office at the Francavilla castle in 1987, was a little girl just before the Second World War. She did not remember Dieu dArakan maybe he had died, because he had been very ill but she recalled perfectly Regina de Rangoon and she had seen the medals won at show, in times past, by the two champions of beauty. The servants and gardeners had been responsible for looking after the cats.

SP. Anyway, Marcel Baudoin was positive that his cats had been sold to Princess Ratibor Hohenlohe, at Satirana Castle, at Lomellina-Pavie.

GB. A strange story, Marcel Reney or rather Marcel Chimonin, because Reney was his Pseudonym-was the general secretary of the Cat Club of Geneva at the time when he bought Rose de Magock and Poupee de Rangoon from Baudoin.

SP.   Abbot Marcel Chamonin had also organised the first cat shows in Switzerland at the beginning of 1933, with the permission of the Cat Club of Paris and the Cat Club of Champagne. Finally, in 1952, the Cat Club of Geneva became independent: when I began my breeding program it maintained its own book of origins.

GB.   When he wrote his book, Abbot Chamonin was the judge of the International Federation of Cats in Switzerland. He loved his cats enormously. He would speak of them at length to his friends, who remembered in particular Poupee de Rangoon, Rose de Magock, Kebir and Fakir de la Chesnaie, Sinh de Saint-Hubert (bought in Belgium from Mlle Rousselle) and a pretty girl Fatima de la Chesnaie. His cats came to a very sad end and an emotional upheaval for Abbot Chamonin. Fatima pined to death after the sudden death of Fakir, the handsome stud, Chamonin's remaining Birmans tragically departed life during a fire at his home.

SP.   In his book of 1947, *Nos Amis Les Chats* (Our Cat friends') Written under the Pseudonym Marcel Reney, he wrote that the Belgian and Swiss breeders involved with the Birman cat had not managed to rescue the breed during the war.

GB. Unfortunately not, on the other hand the French breed structured itself very well, I think, after 1939.

SP. Towards the end of 1933, the Central Feline Society of France and the reunited Cat Clubs of Paris and Champagne, got together and formed the French Feline Federation (FFF) presided over by M Maurice Guingand. There was only one book of origins, for which the Cat Club of Paris was responsible. At this time the registration of suffices became widespread. Mlle Boyer registered hers, Kaabaa, in 1935 at the Central Feline Society. Mme Chaumont-Doisy recovered the name De Madalpour but her breeding suffix had nothing in common with the original Madalpour stock. Moreover, this suffix had been recovered three times by a member of Felikat, a Dutch club it had been registered by the International Cat Federation in 1972.

GB. With the Dutch spelling, I suppose.

SP. Yes, it was Madalpoer's. We are now far away from the Manou de Madalpour of Marcelle Adam.

GB. To resume, French cat breeding was in full-blown expansion in 1935. Moreover, *Vie a la Campagne* published a special edition that year, in which the Birman cat achieved a place of honour.

SP. There was a long article written by Marcel Baudoin-Crevoisier, rehashed in one specialist magazine.

GB.   One finds in this edition a lyrical piece by Mme Chaumont-Doisy, who speaks for the first time about the bearing and above all, the voice of the Birman.

SP.   That's right. As she had begun by breeding Siamese cats, she knew them well and she wrote on the subject of the Birman: "If he has diverted, to his advantage, the admiration which I have for Siamese cats, it is because he does not cry and he is less boisterous. He is mischievous enough, but in a more subtle way. It is difficult to recount all his charm: it is not possible to describe it exactly as it is, but for the last five years, I have been under his charm with a complete pleasure which never fades,"

GB.   Mme Chaumont-Doisy also made a very amusing comparison between her husband and that of her Birmans! When she is running late with dinner, her husband grumbles at her. Whilst Allah, one of her Birmans, becomes very affectionate and rubs himself tenderly round her legs: "the later I am" she says "the more caresses I receive, Birman cats are less selfish than men!"

SP.   That is well known! One moans because he has not had his dinner and the other gives out great affection in order to have it.

GB.   The feline method is much nicer! In reality, poor Birman cats and others went on five years later, to have great problems obtaining their food, like all average French people.

SP. It was the war. Most of the breed disappeared. Mme Ravel who had Succeeded Mlle Tsaut in 1934, remembers how, one Christmas long ago, someone had stolen Farquar Jungo an Abassinian, in order to make, in all likelihood , a stew.

GB. Mlle Boyer deprived herself so that her cats would survive.

SP. It could not have been easy. Her stud Fly de Kaabaa died in 1941 and her girl Miarka died the same year. Orloff was born in 1943 to Micky and Baker, a son and daughter of Fly. It was because of the courage of Mlle Boyer that I decided to work on the breed in my turn.

A moving picture, taken at the end of the war
1945: Madeleine Boyer with Orloff de Kaabaa

THE BIRMAN CAT, A SACRED ANIMAL

This text, relates to the very romantic beginnings of the Birman cat. It is an extract from an article that appeared in *Vie a La Campagne* in October 1926. Poupee de Madalpour, the starting point of the breed, had been shown at the International Cat Show organised by the Cat Club of France in Paris on the 14th and 15th May 1926. The article is signed by Phillippe Jumaud a veterinary surgeon, he was the general secretary of the Cat Club of France and Belgium.

The Birman cat originated in the Far East, the cats of this breed were raised in temples, strictly guarded, and their removal was forbidden. However, after a few years, a pair were imported by Mme Thadde-Hadish (a pair who would provide the basis of the Madalpour line.) These two were in all likelihood stolen by a servant of the temple, who had been dazzled by promises and would take flight in order to avoid punishment. Those who know the fanaticism of Hindus would never think that some priest had been bribed for a fabulous prize: a pair of their sacred animals. Major Sir Russell Gordon, having left the British Army charged with protecting the Kittahs, had, in 1898, the chance to observe these sacred animals. Here are some of his notes…

"Really I think and the learned explorer August Pavie agrees with me that the Siamese cat is a cross between a Birman cat and some Annamite cats imported, in the 17th Century,

into the Khmer Empire. At the time when the swift decline of that empire had closed off the area due to the action of the Thais (Siamese) and the Annamites. In the 6th Century, the Thais had invaded the Khmers and extended power at their expense. The Khmers had consistently resisted the influence of the Indians and Brahmans. Their completely closed religion was consecrated by the powerful and venerated priests the Kittahs. These priests were mercilessly massacred and beaten by the Brahmans until the second Thai invasion at the beginning of the 18ith Century. Those who managed to escape hid in the North of Burma, amongst the impassable mountains. There they founded the underground temple of Lao-Tsun (the dwelling of the gods).

The temple of Lao-Tsun was unquestionably one of the curious marvels of India, which mortals have rarely seen. It is situated on Lake Indaougji between Mogaung and Sembo, in a region almost barren, with barriers of impassable cliffs. There the last Kittahs still lived in 1898 and as a great favour I was granted permission to observe them for a while, with their sacred animals. Following the rebellion and after the English occupation, based at Bhamo, a very isolated place on account of its distance from Mandalay, we protected the Kittahs against a Brahman invasion. We had saved them from certain massacre and pillaging. Their Lama-Kittah, Yotag, welcomed me and presented me with a plaque with a representation of a sacred cat at the feet of a strange divinity, whose eyes were made of two elongated sapphires (item 4108 in my Mildenhall collection). Afterwards he gave me the signal honour of granting me permission to view the sacred cats, numbering about one hundred. He went on to explain their origin to me.

DREAM AND REALITY

The area where Philippe Jumaud placed the legendary temple is in Northeast Burma, near Mogaung and Myitkina, not far from the Chinese border. This region is difficult to access today as it is situated in the Kachin state of the Burma Union. According to Guy Lubeigt, a researcher at CNRS, in charge of the mission in Burma, where he had lived and studied for the preceding eighteen years, in 1898 the Kechin area was perfectly calm and there was no trace of "Brahman Invasions" …Coming from where? It is understood that India was under British rule at that time. Furthermore, the Pavie mission, which explored the valley of the high Mekong (Cambodia and Laos), appeared not to have penetrated very far into Burma. M. Lubeigt also recalled that there were no "Lamas" in Burma "where tantric Buddhism had disappeared in the 18th Century. A minority of Burmans carried the name *Podgi* or *seyado* (venerable, superior, abbot)." He added that the Lao-Tsun temple had never existed in Burma, and the cat was neither sacred nor protected in that country. M Lubeigt says: this is perhaps due to the fact that, in all his previous animal lives Bodhisattva Gautama (who became Buddha) had never been a cat and he had lived in the form of sixteen other animal species (elephant, horse, buffalo, peacock, etc.)" and there is the historic truth. There now follows the story of Sinh, which reads as a pretty tale and has no other pretension, sixteen years after the appearance of the first "Birman Cat" in cat shows.

THE STORY OF SINH, THE SACRED CAT

THE BIRMAN LEGEND

Many versions of this story are in circulation. This one is the very first, extracted from the work of Marcel Reney: The story had been told to him, by Marcelle Adams, who was secretary of the syndicate of French romantic novelists.

Once upon a time in a temple built on the side of Lugh Mountain, lived in prayer, the very venerable Kittah Mun-Ha. He was the Grand Lama precious amongst the precious. The very one for whom the god Song-Hio himself had plaited a golden beard.

There was not one minute, not one look, no one thought, in his existence, which was not devoted to worshipping, to gazing upon, or in the pious service of Tsun-Kyankse. She was the goddess with sapphire eyes, who watched over the transmutation of souls that allowed the Kittahs to live again in the sacred animal for the duration of their animal life, before reclaiming a body hallowed with complete perfection and blessed amongst great priests. Near him meditated Sinh, his dear oracle, a cat completely white, with yellow eyes, which reflected the golden beard of his master and the bronzed body of the goddess with the sky-blue eyes. Sinh the cat councillor, whose ears, nose, tail and tips of his limbs had the tanned colour of the sun, marked with the stain of impurity of all those who touch or are able to touch the earth.

One evening, the malevolent moon allowed the cursed Phoums, abhorred by Siam, to gain entrance. As they drew near to the sacred enclosure, the High Priest Mun-Ha, never ceasing his prayers against the cruel destinies, painlessly entered death, his divine cat by his side and before the despair in the eyes of all his Kittahs, who were overwhelmed.

It was then that the miracle occurred, the unique miracle of immediate transmutation: in a bound, Sinh who was on the golden throne perched upon the head of his collapsed master. He pressed up against his head, weighted down with the years and which for the first time no longer looked upon his goddess. As he remained in his turn rooted to the spot in front of the eternal statue, the bristling white hairs on his spine suddenly turned golden yellow. His golden eyes became blue, like the eyes of the goddess and as he turned his head towards the south gate, his four paws, which had touched the venerable head, became a clear white. His fur became silky like the silk of the sacred vestments. As his eyes turned away from the south gate, the Kittahs, obedient to this demanding gaze charged with strength and light, moved even more quickly to close the heavy bronze gates against the first invasion. The temple was saved from desecration and pillage.

Sinh however, did not leave the throne and on the seventh day, after not moving at all, he turned to the goddess, and looking directly into her eyes, he mysteriously died, carrying to Tsun-Kyankase the spirit of Mun-Ha, too perfect from that moment, for earth.

Seven days later, as the priests gathered to consult with each other in front of the statue, to decide upon a successor of Mun-Ha, all the temple cats rushed in. They were all robed in gold and gloved in white and all their yellow eyes had become a surreal sapphire blue colour. In silence they all surrounded the youngest of the Kittahs and in the same way they had indicated the ancestors who had been reincarnated by the will of the goddess.

Now the storyteller will clarify that what killed a sacred cat in the temple of Lao-Tsun was the spirit of a Kittah, which regained forever his place in heaven with Song-Hio, the god of gold. She concludes that there will also be misfortune for the man who hastens the death of one of those marvellous animals, even if it is unintentional. He will suffer the most-cruel torments until he assuages, with punishment, the spirit which he had perturbed.

Arlette Poirier holding dear old Orloff de Kaabaa

CHAPTER 2

THE REVIVAL OF THE
SACRED CAT OF BURMA

Gisele Barnay.   The situation of the Birman cat after the war was not brilliant. In Switzerland, Belgium and Italy, none had survived. In France they were not flourishing despite the sacrifices made by two or three breeders.

Simone Poirier.   Mme Chaumont-Doisy was able to save some Birmans at her home in Clamart, in the Parisian region. Mlle Boyer had retreated to Millau, in Aveyron, during the war. It was there that a little marvel was born in 1943: Orloff de Kaabaa. Mme Vandalle, who was interested in Birmans around the same time as me, also had a house in Aveyron. We became friends and I met Mlle Boyer through her, two years after the beginning of my breeding program.

GB. Tell me how you began.

SP. At Mme de Maubou's house, there was a little cat in one of the litters of Agni and Aicha de Kaabaa, who she thought was less perfect than the others: she sold it to me at a cheaper price 12,000 francs. My first Birman was called Cosima des Muses, born on 19th April 1953. I bought her in October, at six months old.

GB. Was she pretty?

SP. Yes, she was very pretty: eggshell colouring with seal point markings. She had beautiful eyes of a very strong blue. She did not have perfect gloves because her rear paws did not finish in the points required today but for the time she had quite good gloves. Cosima had a pedigree from the Cat Club going back only two generations, it was an established pedigree for the time. I became a member of the Cat Club and the Countess of Maubou encouraged me to show Cosima at cat shows.

GB. Perhaps she had sold you the cat a little cheaply because she thought her not as perfect as her own.

SP. Maybe…she did believe that a Birman should have a more elongated head. When I showed Cosima at the Cat Club show in October 1953, she won a CAC (*see the certificates of the champions chapter 7*) She corresponded well to the standard, with her round head, her pretty mid-length fur and her very beautiful eyes. The demands on correct gloving were less than they are today. The standards have evolved.

GB.   Tell me a little about the cat shows of 1953.

SP.   The big shows of the Cat Club of Paris were located at the Hotel Continental, in the Rue de Rivoli. Only five cages of Birman cats competed and it was said that the breed had only slightly developed. There were far fewer clubs than there are today. The main clubs were the Cat Circle, created by Baron de Saint-Palais in 1952 and the French Feline Federation to which the Cat Club of Paris belonged: Mme Ravel had been the general secretary since 1934, but a "Cat club" had been in existence for forty years.

GB.   Did you place a bronze Buddha and incense sticks in your cages, like Marcelle Adam did in 1927?

SP.   No! Mme Ravel never accepted decorated cages. All the cats had to be impersonal. She only allowed white linings and she was right: it was much more harmonious.

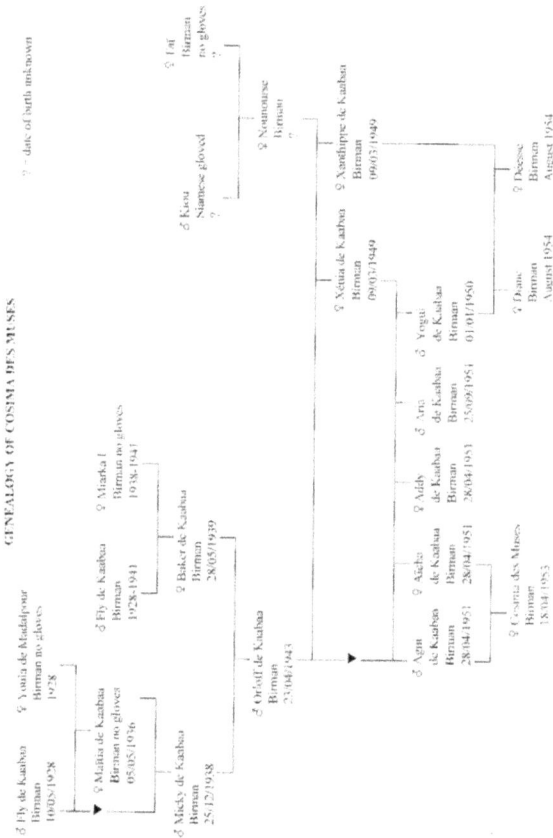

GENEALOGY OF COSIMA DES MUSES

♀ – date of birth unknown

♀ Ply de Kaabaa
Birman
1903/1928

♀ Youla de Madalpour
Birman no gloves
1928

♀ Manou de Kaabaa
Birman no gloves
05/05/1936

♂ Micky de Kaabaa
Birman
26/12/1938

♂ Fly de Kaabaa
Birman
1928-1941

♀ Miarka I
Birman no gloves
1938-1941

♀ Baker de Kaabaa
Birman
28/05/1939

♂ Kiou
Siamese gloved

♀ Loï
Birman
no gloves

♀ Noumoune
Birman

♀ Xenia de Kaabaa
Birman
09/07/1949

♀ Xandhippe de Kaabaa
Birman
09/07/1949

♂ Orloff de Kaabaa
Birman
23/04/1943

♂ Agni
de Kaabaa
Birman
28/04/1951

♀ Aïcha
de Kaabaa
Birman
28/04/1951

♀ Aïdy
de Kaabaa
Birman
28/04/1951

♂ Aro
de Kaabaa
Birman
25/09/1951

♂ Yogui
de Kaabaa
Birman
01/01/1960

♀ Déesse
Birman
August 1954

♀ Déesse
Birman
August 1954

♀ Cosima des Muses
Birman
18/04/1953

Genealogy of Cosima Des Muses

GB. Cosima des Musses was the daughter of Agni and

Achia de Kaabaa, who came from the breeding program of Mlle Boyer. She is therefore the granddaughter of Orloff and Xenia de Kaabaa two prestigious champions.

SP.   Exactly but Orloff was actually her grandfather and her great grandfather because he had mated his daughter Xenia, born in 1949. Not long ago I was able to find the notes Mlle Boyer made just after the war around 1955. She gave us permission to produce a replica of Cosima's pedigree going back six generations.

GB.   Because there had been errors in the replication of pedigrees, certain cats were not included in the Cat Club's Book of Origins. Furthermore some precious documents were destroyed during the war.

When one reads Cosima's authentic pedigree, it strikes you that Mlle Boyer had followed some of Marcel Baudoin-Crevoisier's advice from the Thirties. Nounourse, the mother of Xenia and Xanthippe de Kaabaa, two cats which one finds on most pedigrees were apparently the offspring of a male, gloved, Siamese, this cat had a round head like Yago mated to a Birman female without gloves but with a beautiful mid length coat.

SP.   It would seem so. In 1953, Birman cats sometimes had a morphology a little too Siamese, as did many of the first descendants of Poupee but they always had good gloves.

GB.   Mme Ravel, in the first edition of her book *Le Chat* (The Cat) published in 1955, she wrote that the war had dealt a mortal blow to the Birman breed.

"Which had debased it self by out-crossing with Siamese. Although the paws were whiter the shape of the head and the texture of the fur were completely altered." She added "Some breeders are trying to restore the cat to its original beauty and we sincerely hope that their meritorious efforts will be crowned with success" She was obviously speaking about you.

SP.   Yes, without doubt and also my friend Mme Vandalle, as I did not work alone. There was much work involved to restore the breed without losing its gloves. However in 1953 and 1954 I was happy to show Cosima at the Cat Club shows.

GB.   Did she do well in the competitions?

SP.   Initially yes, Cosima won first CAC's at the Paris show in1953 and again in 1954. And one at Avignon in May 1955 and a prize of honour for her litter of kittens "with long fur." At that time Birmans were judged with the Persians in the longhaired category. She had mated to Zittang des Brosses, a beautiful seal point Khmer from Germany, owned by Mlle Maillard. Everything was going well until then.

The next cat show was at Limoges in August. I made the error of many novices: I took Cosima with her litter of kittens. She was not in very good condition, physically: she was very thin. Despite all that could be done, that summer the cats lost their fur! Mme Guingand the vice president of the French Feline Federation swiftly disqualified her.

Mme Guingand was an international judge and she had known Birman cats from before the war. She said "Your cat is not a Birman!" She was an intelligent woman. She knew that Birman breeding was difficult at that time. She tried to discourage me. She said "You should not have come this far, it is too complicated. Abandon this breed" I knew it was bad, it was for that reason I persevered. Up until then, I hadn't a single ambition, but this would not defeat me."

GB.   You have character. Marcel Baudoin lacked the character with which to carry on.

SP.   Above all, I did not base my hopes on chance! I essentially wanted to restore the breed. To rediscover the style of the beautiful sacred cat of Burma of the thirties, with Dieu d'Arakan as an example, I embarked on the breeding program. With Cosima and her daughter Dorothee, the offspring of Zittang des Brosses, a beautiful Khmer seal point, I tried some out crosses to make the breed better and to achieve perfection. The aims were to regain the rounder style, the silkier quality of the fur, keep those very blue eyes and to try to sort out the gloves as much as possible.

GB.   You did not conceal your out crosses with longhaired cats as the first breeders did.

SP. No, but I was extremely prudent. Dorothee, born on the 16th August 1954 was a ravishing seal point Birman with good gloves. She had her first litter at the age of one: three little white cats of which one Eve had a very pretty coat and blue-green eyes. Her father was Calin des Princes, a white Persian with blue eyes, born of white parents with blue eyes. I only bred from the most beautiful of the three, Eve de Crespieres, much later. Crespieres was my suffix.

GB. You did not want to try anything risky, then: you tried to work intelligently from the beginning?

SP. I am not a theoretician but I was greatly influenced by Mme Ravel. She was a strict woman, who repeatedly said to me: "Look at the pedigrees, gain the knowledge of who their ancestors were and where they came from." I only out-crossed with another breed once.

GB. Who were the descendants of Dorothee.

SP. In her second litter, at the beginning of 1956, she gave birth to two very pretty females with good gloves: Fanchon and Fossette. This time the father was a seal point Birman, the half brother of Dorothee by her father Zittang des Brosses. He was called Cattleya des Muses: his gloves were not perfect, but their style was good.

Fossette went to the home of Marc Doelnitz and teamed with Tabou de Saint-Germain-des Pres like Juliette Greco and Boris Vian. He called Fossette "Plume" and took her everywhere with him: she walked on a lead and peed in the gutter like a dog. The reprisals were that she peed on pillows and for the birth of her kittens she wanted a drawer in the chest of drawers lined with multicoloured boas from Marabou.

GB. Did you have a stud cat at your home for mating your cats.

SP. I bought one, Aria de Kaabaa from Mlle Boyer in 1956. It was Mme Vandalle who introduced us because her two cats Diane and Deesse de Kaabaa, born in August 1954, were the daughters of Xanthippe and Yogui de Kaabaa, who were from Mlle Boyer's breeding program. Aria de Kaabaa was the son of Orloff and Xenia de Kaabaa. I trusted Mme Vandalle and all the breeders she recommended. Mlle Boyer had a very good reputation, as with Baudoin one could judge her by her results. Anyway, I mated Cosima to Aria and she delivered four beautiful kittens at the end of June 1956: two males and two females. Mlle Boyer took some kittens from the litter and their parents.

GB. I found a charming and interesting letter she had written to you at that time: "I hope that Aria will always do well in the country: Bluette, a beautiful fickle infant consoles herself with dear old Orloff." One learns that Orloff, at thirteen, is still alive and has the bearing of a charming man!

SP.   Bluette de Kaabaa, born in February 1952 was also a daughter of Orloff and Xenia. Aria was six months older than she was.

GB.   Aria came to your "stables" again to make babies with Dorothee, amongst others didn't he?

SP.   Yes! But Dorothee De Crespieres no longer belonged to me. I had sold her to another Breeder Mme Battung. As part of our sale agreement, I would have her mated one more time, at my own expense, with Aria and I would keep two kittens from the litter.

The little ones were born on the 1st September 1956. I took Fanfan, a gentle male, to give to a friend and Folie an almost perfect cat to use for breeding. Her eyes were a startling blue and her fur was exceptional very silky. Furthermore Folie was adorable and cuddly. My daughter took her to live at her house. Folie de Crespieres gave birth to beautiful kittens; she also became an international champion.

GB.   In fact Dorothee had only one union with Calin de Princes, the white Persian, you never mated him later with her daughter Eve?

SP.   No of course not. He was only used once. Breeders who do too many out crosses with Persians, whether a single colour or a colour point, obtain Birmans with a short nose with a "stop" The Birman cat has to have the right nose with a very slight stop.

It is necessary to judge everything together: a broad head, a beautiful nose, a mid length silky coat and balanced gloves. Perfect gloves are beautiful and difficult to obtain but they are not enough alone to make a cat of quality.

All these reasons made me very careful. My direction always was, not to mix the breeds, with the one exception. So that better characteristics were obtained for eye colour, glove style and fur. To also limit the number of matings between blood relations, which are inevitable amongst pure bred animals.

GB.   Did you keep the best kittens?

SP.   Yes, but I only kept one or two perfect or near perfect examples. The others were neutered and given to friends. This was always the situation when performing an out cross.

GB.   Eve, who included some well gloved Birmans amongst her ancestors, had white gloves from what geneticists call the "ghost" gene, and were invisible against her completely white coat.

SP.   It was essential that she pass them on to her offspring! Whilst waiting to find a mate worthy of her, I kept her on and I continued with my breeding. I was totally committed and Mme Ravel encouraged me. She was an international judge and travelled greatly. Each time she saw whilst abroad, an interesting new breed, she ordered a cat for me! I would go to the airport to collect it. She sent me two superb Persian Chinchillas in this way but I did not keep them because they did not get on with my cats.

In June 1957, I had boarding with me, Briarry Carazal a beautiful seal Colourpoint Persian aged one, bought from Brian Sterling-Webb, who had worked with the breed for seven years, he had shown it in England in 1955. My friend Mme Gamichon was interested in the Colourpoint and we frequently collaborated, just as I did with Mme Vandalle. I bought three more beautiful female cats, two blue and one seal, but gradually Mme Vandalle and I decided to only breed Birmans, so I gave all my Colourpoints to Mme Gamichon.

GB. You also introduced the Burmese cat to France.

SP. Yes, through Mme Ravel the same year. I received Nilgiris Buri Atakata, the first female Burmese Zibeline imported into France. As you know, it was to avoid confusion with the English Burmese that our Birman officially called itself "the sacred cat of Burma" from 1950.

GB. Did you have a large apartment to hold all these cats?

SP. When one breed's cats, it is necessary to have space and time, profit must not be the number one priority. I did not have many holidays during those years and I spent a lot of money. I had an artist's studio, which was my husband's: he was the director of an advertising agency and also a painter.

The apartment had a gallery and a long Mezzanine. There I built a grilled cage measuring two metres by two and a half metres and three metres high. Into this cage I placed cats that needed to be isolated, a litter for example, or others. I had almost twenty-five cats at that time; all of them kittens, which required a lot of care and attention. Luckily, my daughter and my friends came to help me. I was at that time a director of my husband's advertising agency. I had worked for the promotion for fifteen years. God be thanked, the offices were in the same building as the apartment where my cats lived, as I would not have given them up.

GB.   Did your breeding go well?

SP.   I had good and bad moments, pleasant surprises and difficult periods. I soldiered on. The Birman cat really was my passion. As early as 1957 the first blue point Birman appeared in a cat show in Paris. It was a notable moment in the feline world! I went to see him, he was presented at a cat show organised by the Friends of Cats. This club had existed since 1936, I think: it had become active after the war but did not organise regular shows. The club had disbanded at the end of the Fifties; a friend of Jean Cocteau Mme Andree Peyraud had run it.

GB.   Jean Cocteau loved many cats and some more than himself.

SP.   He had designed a logo for the Friends of Cats, by which it is best remembered. Anyway, I had come to admire this three and a half months old blue Birman kitten, Gastounet de Madalpour. He came from the breeding stock of Mme Chaumont-Doisy, a member of the Friends of Cats. It was said that she had crossed her Birmans with some blue Persians and I wanted to see the result.

This cat interested me, but I was not in a position to buy it: Mme Chaumont-Doisy wanted 50,000 francs for him. He was bought by a friend who renamed him Gounalankara, as this was a much nobler name for a sacred cat of Burma. To conclude Gounalankara never had any descendants, either blue point or seal. As for me I always wanted a cat with the blue gene from Mme Chaumont-Doisy.

Whilst waiting, I had other things on my mind. 1958 was a sad year: it was then that Cosima died. I had problems with her, starting with an ear infection and a chronic head cold. We cared for her and she was well for a year. She had given birth to four very beautiful litters of kittens, but in October 1957, her labour did not go very well. I was only able to save one of the two newly born kittens. I worried about it.

GB. It is necessary to allow for illnesses too, in a breeding program…

SP. Alas yes! Mainly from those which others bring to you. At the end of 1955, a breeder who I will not name asked me if I would allow Cosima to breast-feed a litter of kittens for her, at the same time as her own litter. I was not careful enough: all the kittens had ringworm. A disaster! I saved one of them all the others died.

At that time, there was no effective medication. One had to cover the cats with a tincture of iodine, which burned them. If it did not finish them off. After this episode I was afraid of everything, especially fleas and illnesses. When someone brought me a Queen for a mating, I examined it thoroughly.

Cosima was saved, but she remained fragile and it was necessary to give her lots of attention. She died, in March 1958 at the age of five, from a very sad illness that lasted for many months. She had a number of abscesses, including one on her anus, which caused her enormous suffering. She did not seem to understand me any more. It was painful and profoundly sad not to be able to relieve her suffering. I was very greatly affected…

GB. The death of a loved animal is always difficult to bear but you also knew good moments. It seems to me that a passion like yours is somewhat like that of a collector of objets d'art, always searching for the perfect piece.

SP. That is possible. When Mme Vandalle and I learned that Mme Chaumont-Doisy was going to sell her whole breeding stock, we immediately reserved the cats and went to collect them. Nothing would have held us back.

What an adventure! It was January 1959. It was cold enough to crack stone and we were still in discussions. Mme Chaumont-Doisy, very old and ill had been moved to her son's house in the Parisian region. She had always lived at Clamart and all her cats had been entrusted to a neighbour, whilst waiting to be re homed. We discussed the purchase with Mme Chaumont-Doisy's son.

Sweet International Champion Fantine

We then took the train, wrapped up warmly and carrying a heap of travelling boxes to hold our cats! At the neighbours house there were twenty Birmans, one of them Eloi-Eryx a splendid seal point and Fantine. I took these, the two most beautiful: Eloi would be another male for my breeding program. Mme Vandalle took three others; one of them was Caline-Cathou de Madalpour, the mother of Eloi- Eryx.

Fantine, a ravishing seal point Birman, was the daughter of Caline-Cathou and Eloi Eryx. It was I who called her Fantine. She did not have a name or an official pedigree. She was in any case the sister of Gastounet de Madalpour, perhaps born in the same litter, in 1957.

GB. I suppose what attracted both you and Mme Vandalle, was the hope of seeing the birth of blue Birmans using Caline-Cathou and Eloi-Eryx?

SP. We had already begun to breed from these two cats. We were returning by train, with the pair of them plus our five cats in the travelling boxes, when Fantine gave birth to two kittens! We wrapped the mother and the newly born kittens in soft blankets, to keep them warm. Unfortunately the little girl died, so I was only able to breed from the male.

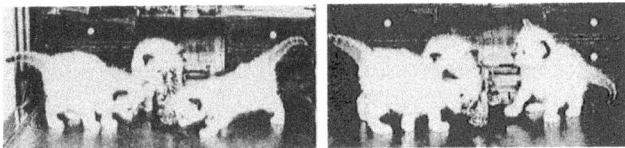

Three of Fantine's kittens intrigued with an automaton.

GB. Do you think that, blue Persians transmitted the famous blue gene?

SP. There was no way of creating the blue Birman without the blue gene carried by blue Persians or Khmers. Mme Chaumont-Doisy was a friend of Mme Gillet, a civil servant from Cambodia, who bred three breeds: seal Birmans, blue Khmers and Persians. One could presume from her results that she had performed out crosses.

GB. Mme Chaumont-Doisy bought a seal point Birman stud from Mlle Boyer, called Yogui de Kaabaa. In her diaries Mlle Boyer wrote that the Birmans of Mme Chaumont had very good gloves after she had acquired Yogui.

SP. It is true Mme Chaumont-Doisy's cats were superb but she wasn't only interested in the gloves. On reflection, she did much to improve glove style.

GB. The result of the union of the two families produced magnificent offspring, which can be found in almost every current pedigree. The Madalpour family (of Mme Chaumont-Doisy, not to be confused with those of Marcelle Adam) and the Kaabaa family were united for the betterment of the breed! Caline-Cathou, bought by Mme Vandalle, was I think the daughter of Yogui de Kaabaa.

SP. She was indeed the daughter of Yogui de Kaabaa and Hebe de Madalpour. It was Hebe who provided the blue gene.

GB. In 1959, you had two beautiful stud cats, Aria de Kaabaa and Eloi-Eryx de Madalpour. Where did you keep them? Stud cats mark their territory, they spray.

SP. I never kept them at home. My stud cats lodged with another breeder, Mme Millet. I only kept female cats and Kittens at home.

GB. The stud cats came along at a good time.

SP. Very much so, Eloi-Eryx was introduced into my experiments and mated to Eve de Crespieres, my pretty white cat, the daughter of Dorothee de Crespieres and Calin des Princes.

GB. Did the kittens take after their father or mother?

SP. Neither, Jumbo de Crespieres was born in 1960. He had a superb black coat and four perfect white gloves. The following year the same mating produced Kora de Crespieres. She resembled her elder brother: black with a beautiful semi longhaired coat. She had golden eyes and white gloves. Another black female, not as well gloved, I gave to my vet, who neutered her.

GB. One decision astonishes me: before the war and before you began your breeding, the cats were recorded in the French book of Feline Origins (LFOF), as Birman or Siamese etc. even if their parents, not recorded therein, were of another breed.

Kora de Crespiers
daughter of Eve de Crespiers a Blue Eyed White Persian

Pedigree of:

KORA DE CRESPIERES

Date of Birth: 4.4.1981 Sex: Female Breed:
Colour & Markings: Black with white feet Reg No.: RIEX 404 181 0021
Owned By: Mrs Gertrude Griswold Bred By: Mme Simone Poirier

PARENTS	GRANDPARENTS	GREAT GRANDPARENTS	GREAT GREAT GRANDPARENTS
SIRE: INT CH ELOI ERYX DE MADALPOUR Reg No.: LOF RIEX 1853 Colour: Seal Point DOB: 1.1.1955	YOGUI DE KAABAA LOF 2854 DOB: 1.5.1950 CALINE CATHOU DE MADALPOUR LOF 1547 DOB: 1.1.1953	CH ORLOFF DE KAABAA LOF 2190 Seal Point	MICKY DE KAABAA LOF
			BAKER DE KAABAA LOF 2188
		INT CH XENIA DE KAABAA LOF 2812 Seal Point	CH ORLOFF DE KAABAA LOF 2190
			NOUNOURSE DE MON SOURIS
		YOGUI DE KAABAA LOF 2854 Seal Point	CH ORLOFF DE KAABAA LOF 2190
			INT CH XENIA DE KAABAA LOF 2812
		HEBE DE MADALPOUR LOF 1187 Seal Point	LUI A MOI DE MADALPOUR
			PRINCESSE DE MADALPOUR LOF 824
DAM: EVE DE CRESPIERES Reg No.: LOF RIEX 1 Colour: Blue Eyed White DOB: 2.8.1955	CH CALIN DES PRINCES LOF 3815 2A DOROTHEE DE CRESPIERES LOF 4233 DOB: 16.8.1964	CH YOUNG DES PRINCES LOF 2803 2A Blue Eyed White	CH SOUTHWAY RASCAL LOF 2785
			NETHEREDGE SNOW STORM LOF 2064 2A
		NETHEREDGE SNOW STORM LOF 2064 2A Blue Eyed White	NETHEREDGE PIMMS 39218
			NETHEREDGE SNOW FAIRY GCCF 2
		ZITTANS DES BROSSES LOF 29742BN-2799BD Khmer	GNIOUF VON FROHNAU LO DEUTCH 274
			VANSITTHI VON IRAK ADSCHEMI LO DEUTCH 273
		COSIMA DES MUSES LOF 3658 Seal Point	AGNI DE KAABAA LOF 3110
			AICHA DE KAABAA LOF 3111

I the undersigned do hereby certify that the foregoing particulars are correct to the best of my knowledge and belief.

SIGNED DATE

Kora's pedigree
(This was not printed in the original book)

SP. Effectively yes. To enrol in the LFOF one only needed to make a simple declaration as to the appearance of the cat. The French Federation, under the impetus of Mme Ravel, wanted their book of origins, to be like the book of origins of the International Federation. To be registered in these books one had to have a minimum of three pure generations.

The Book of Origins of the Cat Club was put together in 1946, by collecting together three books: that of the Cat Club of Paris and its region, The Central Feline Society and the Cat Club of Champagne. There was a second book too started in 1958: it was a register for pending and screening of new breeds, the RIEX. This first, experimental register was obligatory and delivered by the International Feline Federation of Europe, at their general meeting at Copenhagen in 1958 to all the international clubs. The cats whose parents or grandparents were of another breed would appear in this register. The Birman cat, for example, would achieve entrance to the LFOF (or LOF for short) after three generations of cats with the Birman Phenotype, in principle, after approval in a cat show (Novice Class). Two international judges named by the FIFe could also give the approval.

GB. From this time, all the cats bred from a cross were only registered in the LOF as Birmans on the third generation.

SP.   The offspring of Eve de Crespieres, Jumbo and Kora were of course registered on the RIEX. For one of the other books it was necessary to provide a mating certificate, signed by the owner of the stud cat and a birth certificate, signed by the owner of the cat. Naturally, the breeders had to respect the letter of the year, when naming their kittens. It made it easier to remember their date of birth.

The offspring of Kora and Jumbo were registered in the RIEX. They were beautiful. I had already mated Kora, my beautiful "Birman in negative" with Jumbo. One of their kittens Marquis de Crespieres was born in April 1963. He was a seal point Birman with perfect gloves and good type. I then mated Kora to El Dinn de Madalpour, one of Mme Chaumont-Doisy's stud cats owned by Mme de Clerke. From this mating Namour de Crespieres was born on 17th March 1964: another little male cat of good Birman type, a perfect seal point with four well gloved paws.

These two cats Marquis and Namour, were stud cats of the highest order. Always mated to seal or blue Birmans, they always produced "Pure" Birmans, never black ones. Moreover, Marquis was the beginning of a line that is found again and again in many current pedigrees: including that of Koster bred from his daughter Sibylline, born in 1969.

GB.   As I finished my investigations, I checked the

performances of Marquis and Namour in the archives of the Cat Club. They had once again offered their services as stud cats at the beginning of 1975: Namour was eleven years old and Marquis twelve it proves that the breeders were satisfied with their descendants! *Marquis de Crespieres lived in Rouen, with Mme Poplin and Namour de Crespieres lived in Haubourdin with Mlle Pottrain, the president of the Cat Club of Northern France.*

SP. It also proved that Kora, coupled with a "pure" Birman, produced beautiful little kittens. She went to live in the United States and I gave Eve and Jumbo to Mme Gamishon.

GB. The Americans were the first to be interested in the French Birman, but we will come back to that. I can tell you that in 1959 and 1960, Doctor Seipel, of Fairfax Virginia, imported three beautiful cats from France: Irraoudi du Clos Fleuri, a seal point male Josika du Clos Fleuri, a blue female and Joanne D'Ormailley, a seal point female she was the daughter of Deesse and Eros de Madalpour. A fourth male Kairos de Lugh, arrived at Doctor Seipel's home in 1961. These four cats were the grandchildren of Yogui de Kaabaa.

SP. It was always the lines of Madalpour and Kaabaa, at the Feline Circle and similarly at the Cat Club. There was rumour of another line but it was a false road! In 1961, I received a letter from an American Mrs Griswold, who lived in Tacoma. She had been sent a couple of "cats from the temples of Tibet" the previous year. She included a photograph of her cats Pkaa a female and Klaa a male, she also provided the name of the friend who had sold them to her: Mr Townes

Pkaa is on the Left and Klaa on the right

I wrote to Mr Townes in Cambodia, in order to find out where he had obtained these two cats, in the hope of clarifying the Asiatic origin of the Birman cat. The truth was simpler: Mr Townes replied kindly that he had bought the parents of Klaa and Pkaa from Mme Gillet, a French Civil Servant posted to Cambodia! The two cats Bok Khmer and Schiaffa came from her breeding…. All a bit silly.

Carter Townes holding Bok And
Gertrude holding Shiaffa of Asia

Carter Townes and In Dinn holding Bok and Shiaffa

Gertrude Griswold holding Pkaa and Klaa Khmer

GB. They certainly possessed the blood of the blue Persian and the Khmer, who were a type of Colourpoint, bred in France and Germany, before the work of M Brian Stirling-Webb in England. Moreover Mlle Gillet had taken all the Breeding stock from Mme Hanna Krueger, a breeder of Khmers, including some with white feet, like Fandango. This cat was obtained before the Second World War from Mme Von Werner, of Berlin.

In an American newsletter of the "Sacred Cat of Burma Fanciers," Mrs Griswold wrote that her Cambodian cats were not perfectly gloved: "they always keep a little white on their paws and the whole glove has been lost because of an uncontrolled selection."

SP. Everything adds up. Zittang des Brosses also came from Germany. The Khmer improves the Birman, provided it does not do any wild or incorrect intervention so that the gloving is retained. In any case I was very disappointed that I had not found an Asiatic source of the Birman!

At this time, the sacred cat of Burma was still not recognised by the American CFA (Cat Fanciers Association). I suggested to Mrs Griswold that I help her to improve the breed, using the French branch, not the Tibetan! In 1962, I sent her an excellent stud cat aged sixteen months, Korrigan, the son of Eloi-Erix and Hebe de L'Irraouada, a daughter of Aria. At the same time, I sent her a female of six months, Leslie de la Regnardiere, a granddaughter of Eloi-Eryx and my beautiful Fantine.

The condition of sale was that I should receive one kitten from each litter produced. In December 1963, I received Martine of Clover Creek, the daughter of Pkaa and Korrigan (*who became "of Clover Creek"*) and Dablu, the son of Leslie and Klaa. In 1965 another kitten from Korrigan and his daughter Griswold' Belyea arrived: this was my Olympio born on the 21st May. He was the only male cat I kept in my house. In the meantime I sent Kora to Mme Griswold in the United States. We will talk of that later.

GB.   Why did you keep Olympio in your house, contrary to your usual rules of conduct?

SP.   My two stud cats, Aria and Eloi-Eryx, died in 1961. I didn't see them because they lived at Mme Millet's house. The life of a stud cat is not a very happy one: he is isolated in a little "house" or in a cage.

A stud cat will only see a female when mating and he can become a little sexually obsessed, you might say. Anyway I did not want this lifestyle for Olympio. I was lucky he didn't spray. He fathered kittens between 1966 and 1968. Unfortunately he began to mark his territory when I moved to Boulogne to live with my daughter in 1967. He completely wrecked an antique wardrobe!

He finally settled down in the house: I did not have the heart to be separated from him but I did have him castrated. He died from an attack of uraemia in 1972, aged seven.

GB.   The years went by. You founded the Birman Cat Circle and shared your passion with the young.

SP. The "Birman and Colourpoint Cat Circle" was founded in 1961, within the Cat Club of Paris. There were a dozen members, including Mme Ravel, Mme Vandalle, Mme Gamichon and of course Mlle Boyer, my daughter and myself. Our aim was to protect the sacred cat of Burma, helping new breeders to retain their beauty. We knew it was difficult because we had experienced it ourselves.

GB. There is one phrase that often springs to your lips on the subject of certain breeders: "They are Merchants!" What do you mean exactly?

SP. They are the sort who are not interested in the improvement of the breed, but only immediate profit. They care little about destroying the breed that has required years of work to stabilise their characteristics. There are always true clubs of serious breeders but I am not able to approve the others, who mess everything up. I have loved the sacred cat of Burma too much to lose interest in it.

GB. You have created a following. With Francine and Jean-Louis de Pindray at the Cat Club, for instance, the sacred cat of Burma has its perfect protectors.

SP. That's true and I am happy about that. Jean-Louis de Pindray bought his first Birman Ophelie de Pouh-Miloh, at a Cat club show at the end of 1965.

GB. He regarded himself as your spiritual son because

he always asked you for extensive advice and he worked with extreme prudence, just as you did.

SP. Yes and he, along with Mme Lemoine, undertook a huge advertising campaign to promote Birman cats both in France and abroad, at all the cat shows. His cats were splendid. Mme Lemoine only took two cats with her; one was Gipsy, the daughter of Plume de Crespieres, born at the home of Marc Doelnitz.

For us cat shows were a family Fete, everyone took part. Renee Pottrain, the president of the Cat Club of Northern France, owner of Namour de Crespieres had also worked with Francine and Jean-Louis de Pindray. In 1973 Renee offered my daughter a pretty seal point Birman Ines de Pagan. She was a superb show quality cat but we never showed her.

GB. Jean-Louis told me about your team spirit. He found that his way of thinking was completely changed. He may have been a young man but he certainly knew the cat world well as he went on to become an international judge, like your daughter Arlette. He told to me "Twenty years ago, you applauded the winning cat, even if you weren't the owner. Today the breeders sulk, argue and go elsewhere when their cat does not win! It is a competition and it is necessary to take it seriously, but not to transfer that disappointment onto the animal.

SP. I think that this has mentality always existed. Every individual always thinks that his cat, just like his child, is the most beautiful but it is true that we have an astonishing team spirit.

I remember my unique meeting with Marcelle Adam, just after I had started breeding in1956 or perhaps 1957. I was showing Folie at the Cat Club show at the Continental Hotel. She was at that show and I heard her say to a friend who was with her: "These cats are hideous!" That hurt me because I had worked very hard and the cats were beautiful. I did not want to speak to her and that's a shame.

GB. She did not reveal to you any unpublished information regarding the origin of the "cat of Burma," anyway. Perhaps she thought Manou de Madalpour, with his beautiful fur, his slightly Siamese style and his shorter gloves was more beautiful than the Post war Birman cats.

SP. Perhaps, although Dieu d'Arakan, in 1930, already had a very "round" look. He was rather an exception for the period. Orloff and Aria de Kaabaa were like him. Their eyes were of a profound blue, magnificent and have become very rare today.

GB. Today's Birmans often have pale blue eyes. The colour of the iris is very important, I think, in order to become an international champion.

SP.   The eyes have to be sapphire blue but everything has to be taken into account: it is the whole cat that has to be judged.

GB.   Most of your cats have won may fine prizes but I am surprised. At the homes of most of the breeders I have interviewed, I have seen many cups and rosettes on display. In your home nothing is on display they are all in boxes.

SP.   That is true, I am more interested in breeding than showing my cats even though Aria, Eloi-Eryx, Fantine, Folie, Olympio and others have become international champions.

GB.   As did Semele de Mun Ha, you're last Birman who died in 1986 at the age of seventeen.

SP.   Ah! Semele, my sweet blue point Birman she became an international champion in 1972. She was born on 9th April 1969. Gradually I stopped breeding but I do miss it. I am interested in cat shows, I go to every one I can and I still run the Birman Cat Circle, which separated from the colour point club on the 27th October 1984

However, times have changed. The death of friends and cats that I loved mark those last years. Mme Ravel died in 1984; Mlle Boyer preceded her in 1973. Their strict ways seemed old fashioned. I had hoped that the younger members who took over would carry on the good work and not succumb to the whims of fashion. The fashion was to create as many new colours as possible. This required using a variety of breeds, contaminating our beautiful sacred cat of Burma.

I haven't heard anyone say that the tortie point Birman is beautiful: she looks daubed and her gloves not very distinctive. She lacks the essence of the Birman qualities, the beauty, and the mystery... I would be curious to monitor what she passes on to her descendants!

EXTRACTS FROM THE DIARIES OF MADELEINE BOYER

Madeleine Boyer, the daughter of an Admiral, and herself a sailing instructor, bought her first cat, Fly de Kaabaa in 1928. He would be the grandfather of Orloff de Kaabaa; his descendants, allied with those of the Madalpour line of Mme Chaumont-Doisy, today live all over the world. Mlle Boyer kept a sort of diary; it is a document of great assistance in the history, of the breeding, of the sacred cat of Burma. We have been able to recover a few pages of this document:

Fly de Kaabaa was born in Provence at Pre des Pedcheurs. The breeder, Mme Gilles-Lenaerts was not able to give me the pedigree of this young "angora" cat but never the less I bought him. I longed to have a good and pretty pussycat. He was born on the 10th May 1928 and registered in the Book of Origins of the Central Feline Society in 1935.

Each evening when I returned from sea, my boisterous friend was waiting for me. He scratched and bit the sails, as I hastened to submerge my self in the big wooden tub filled with scented water. I gave him some "gavarons" (little fish which fishermen cannot sell) to console him for being an imprisoned demigod, whilst I had known the joys of sailing.

Fly my first Birman, purred himself to sleep on my shoulder whilst I played Chopin's Nocturne on the piano in the evening. When at sea, he was the king of Port Saint-Louis, at Mourillon, where all the fishermen threw their "daily bread" into the dinghy that brought us back to solid ground.

In 1933 I had to give up the mild South of France for various reasons. It was winter when Fly and I were grounded, under snow, in Paris. Fly moved with me to many hotels in Boulevard Bineau, whilst we waited to find a studio between Neuilly and Levallois. It was there, I began to breed Birmans, using Fly and Youla de Madalpour.

Between 1935 and 1936, I lost twelve little kittens, from mating these seven-year-olds.

In April 1936, I moved to Avenue de Breteuil, where despite some troubles, I had the pleasure seeing Fly and

Youla produce four splendid kittens on the 5th May 1936. One of those kittens was Maitia. The lodgings were slightly insalubrious so I moved home again, this time installing myself in a large studio in Avenue Lecourbe. On Christmas Eve 1938, in Provence, a friend and I were listening to the mass of the Holy Virgin on the radio whilst Maitia gave birth to Micky, Vega and Sonia. On the 23rd Naima (a white Siamese with mid-length fur, the daughter of Fly) had given birth to Liang and Futifu.

Miarka 1 (Miquette) was a half Birman purchased in 1938. She bore kittens at the age of nine months. Her kittens were sent to a wet nurse, all except Baker de Kaabaa. In September 1939, I had a number of queens: Maitia, Miarka 1 and Naima. "Miquette" and Fly produced three beautiful kittens that I was not able to take with me when I left Paris for Millau. Mme Constant wrote to me to say she had sold them the moment the great exodus swept to Millau and Perpignan. At Millau, I had to send Micky, my most beautiful male, to the home of Mme Calmes, who owned a beautiful Siamese; and I entrusted Baker to Margurite Raynal. Fly could put up with Liang, who was so mild in temperament but got on very badly with Micky. I lost Miarka1 in June 1941 and Fly in July. That left me with Naima, Maitia and dear Liang, who walked on his back legs like a clever dog. He died on the 31st December 1944.

NB. The cats born during the war at the home of Mlle Boyer in Millau were Youki the son of Maitia and Liang born November 1941. Miarka II the daughter of Baker and Liang was born on the 28th June 1942. Nanky and Minouche, the daughters of Baker and Liang on the 20th November 1942: Orloff, the son of Baker and Micky on the 23rd April 1943. Maitia and Naima died in November and December 1947, Micky and Baker in January and February 1949

CHAPTER 3

A DIFFICULT BREED

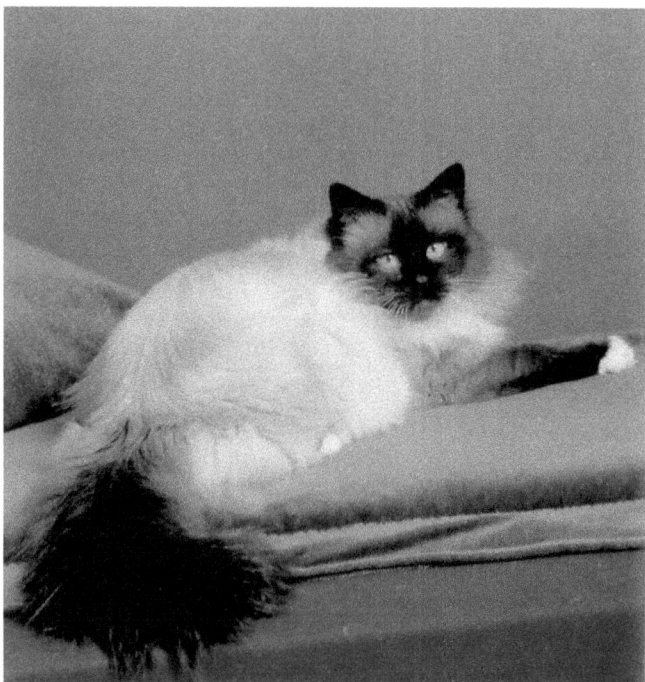

Tresor Lune d'Argent

Gisele Barnay.   When one reads Philippe Jumaud's thesis and then Marcel Baudoin's articles plus Marcel Reney's book, one retraces the whole evolution of the sacred cat of Burma. One is better able to understand the reaction of Marcelle Adam at the show: Manou de Madalpour was not much like Tresor Lune d'Argent The superb seal point stud cat of our cover. He would not become an international champion.

Simone Poirier.   According to Jumaud's standard, the head and the body were more elongated than we see today. He also insisted upon a longer bushy tail and eyes of "Intense royal blue, and very mobile." The gloves were less precisely described. The first standard indicated only that "the face, tail, ears and paws are a darker brown, like an otter. The four paws end with a white glove, stopping beneath the joint.

GB.   Ten years later in 1935, the "perfect prototype" already demanded a "strong, large and round" head. The gloves were a little more detailed. The standard indicated that where the white colouring of the paws was not equal, it was important that there was more white on the back paw then the front:" she must also show the shape of a boot rising higher at the back." In 1947, the famous glove had to stop "in a point" on the rear paw. By 1987, the standard stated the dimensions, which had to be achieved for an ideal point. Is it so important that this amazing cat should have a perfect boot drawn to a point behind his rear paw?

SP. You remind me of the time I met Marcel Baudoin-Crevoisier in 1967. He mocked the "mittens" of the Birman cat of the sixties and "the demi-musketeer gloving forming a point on the back paws!"

If the Birman Cat Circle requested some standards it was because in a cat show the judging of the gloves varied with each judge. In France, shorter points were preferred, whilst in other European Countries of the FIFe, higher points scored better. Basic standards were needed and so at its meeting in July 1986, the International Federation adopted our proposal that the ideal points do not go up further than the back of the Knee joint: they should be quite short. This proposal was passed unanimously.

GB. What happens if a cat is perfect in all other respects is he disqualified if he has a small gloving defect?

SP. Not necessarily! The judges take account of the whole cat. In the beginning the absence of points would not mean disqualification but today they have become necessary for taking part. Additionally, the changes in the standard are most obvious on the subject of the scale of points. (*See Chapter 7*)

GB. What is the scale of points? What does it signify?

SP. It is a way of calculating the quality of the cat according to the importance given to one characteristic or another. For example, in 1955 colouring and gloves were judged together for thirty points. In the last standard of the FIFe, colouring was given fifteen points, front and rear paws five points for each paw, taking their regularity into account (five points) and the points: five points.

GB. When one realises that the famous gloves are passed from one generation to the next with no guarantee of regularity, one can see why breeding the sacred cat of Burma is said to be so difficult! Yes, because even Feline geneticists cannot agree upon the gene responsible for gloving.

Apparently it is a very complex phenomenon, for experienced geneticists and zoologists. Professor Philippe Dreux, who had worked on this issue for a number of years, recognised this: "It is not at all well known how the gene, which gives the irregular colouring, functions. The Birman has a gentle colouring localised on its paws, which appears in an extremely random manner."

SP. It is this that demands that the breeder pays attention to their breeding program: I have tried it! Over the course of five generations of beautiful Birmans with excellent gloves, there were only one or two kittens in each litter, which were absolutely perfect. The others had good gloves but they were not as even. I am pleased that an eminent researcher has confirmed this difficulty.

GB. Jean-Louis de Pindray and other breeders I interviewed confirmed the percentage for this being in the region of 40%, from a study using two hundred kittens born to "pure" parents and grandparents over five or six generations.

SP. This proves that I don't talk a load of drivel when I advise prudence before the inevitable intervention of another, non-gloved, breed. It is very important to supervise the breeding program. I can tell you that two average cats are able to produce beautiful offspring as long as their grandparents were perfect.

GB. We have seen that excessive out crosses with Persians also risk giving the Birman a nose too short and with a "stop"

SP. It also alters the texture of the fur. It becomes less beautiful and woolly. The fur of the sacred cat of Burma is silky and must remain so. Mme Ravel who was a great Persian specialist said to me one day, whilst stroking my cat Semele "It's extraordinary! What a quality coat, it is delightful to stroke fur like this.

GB. Jean-Louis de Pindray told me that the Birman is a very difficult cat to judge. It is necessary to take all the aspects of the cat at the same time: the texture of the fur, the shape of the head, the nose and ears, the colour of the coat with no white spots on the paws. The eyes-not must not be too light and of course without a squint, and finally the gloves, an additional obstacle to clear, in order to obtain the highest distinction. What is your idea of perfection?

SP.   It is the whole cat including its charm. The sacred cat of Burma and you know this since you own one, has an enormous amount of charm. The most beautiful cat is a stocky cat with strong quite short paws. The fur is exceptionally fine, mid length except round the neck where it spreads out like a collar; it ripples in the wind and does not tangle, which is very important. The head is well proportioned, with a strong jaw and a neatly sculptured chin, not at all receding. The Birman has little ears and a marvellous gaze from eyes that are ideally sapphire blue. Fantine had eyes like that. Unfortunately I only have a black and white photograph of her.

GB.   It's a shame but despite that, this photograph gives a very good idea of her beauty. One thing has struck me whenever I see a Birman, that is the way the Birman cat walks, as though it is dancing… it is the only cat to my knowledge that walks this way, with its feet turned slightly outwards like a ballet dancer!

SP.   Baudoin-Crevoisier emphasised the way the sacred cat of Burma walks. He saw it as grace mingled with strength and he thought that this cat and its story would provide an excellent subject for a ballet. The dancers to be dressed in Birman cat costumes. He said this I think because the shape of the points behind the foot also emphasises the "dancing" aspect of the Birman. For all intents and purposes, the cat already has the shoes!

GB. The shoes and the mask these famous dark markings were formerly reserved for the Siamese cat.

SP. It is important not to confuse the Siamese *breed* with the Siamese *gene* responsible for the markings. In certain journals I have often come across some appalling mistakes. The Siamese breed was imported into England in the second half of the Nineteenth Century, before Gregor Mendel's theory of inheritance was discovered.

GB. It was a geneticist who gave the gene the name of the Siamese breed, not the reverse. Moreover, biologists who worked on laboratory mice gave this gene another name *Himalayan* because there are mice with Siamese markings. M Guenet says "There are no laws so you can name a gene as you wish"

Given that this terminology was defined in English, it was possible to standardise and call the gene responsible for the markings points. It was more logical, as the English called the coloured extremities of the Siamese "points"

SP. What does Professor Dreux think about the origin of these markings?

GB. Gene C, which is very important for the colouring,

is able to undergo a certain number of mutations more or less profound, which alter the wild coat. Professor Dreux said that "The appearance of a mutation is very rare, in one sexual cell the chance of seeing this mutation appear is once in a million sperm or ova. One mutation of gene C where only the extremities of the coat are coloured, like the Siamese, made its appearance a long time ago in south east Asia in the wild or semi domesticated cat of Asia. She had been bred in the Far East. (It is a hypothesis, but the characteristic was handed down and stayed)."

(See Chapter 8 for more about genetics. In the original book the text continued here.)

Some very ancient Thai manuscripts are illustrated with pictures of pale cats with Siamese markings. These manuscripts are kept on the National Library, Bangkok. Around 1870 some examples of this particular cat were imported in to Great Britain and the English continued the breeding of the seal point Siamese.

SP.   Today the Siamese is not the only cat to have the coloured mask, ears, paws and tail. There are Persian Colourpoints, the Balinese a Siamese with semi long hair originating in the United States and the Birman who adds the white gloves to his coloured points.

GB.   Packed with sophistication, yet they match a mouse! I have not learned any more about how a seal point mouse with gloves was created. Who knows? Maybe the loss of pigmentation of the extremities is a characteristic that appears spontaneously in most mammals. To make it perfect is another issue but it does not halt progress. Genetic manipulations offer us at present tailor made twin calves and are waiting to offer us some babies conditioned to obey without thinking! The empirical way of traditional breeders was always less worrying.

SP.   I have explained too the methodologies, based on good sense and observation. Rabbit breeding and certain works on the benefits and problems of inbreeding with dogs also inspired me. I have never taken the easy way out.

GB.   Animals were bred before Gregor Mendel's discovery of the mechanics of inheritance. The current researchers don't forget it.

SP.   Mlle Boyer worked in that way. She noted all her breeding results over five or six generations, including a commentary on their style: "one "pure" female with " boots" only on her rear paws, mated with a "pure" male with very good gloves produced two cats (out of four) which had gloves on all four paws"

GB.   Her cats were inevitably very much inbred, as were they all during the war. Orloff was perhaps one successful result. Moreover, she wrote that in order to keep the breed in good health; it was necessary to avoid mating brother and sister, unless they had different mothers. "Unless the subject (always male) shows signs of degeneration one year on," she said.

SP. I knew many new breeders who did mate brother and sister at that time. They inevitably had difficulties: the kittens were very fragile.

GB. Yet Cosima was the daughter of Agni and Aichia, the son and daughter of Orloff and Xenia de Kaabaa in the same litter.

SP. My Cosima was always delicate and she died at the age of five, despite constant care. On the other hand, Kora and Jumbo de Crespieres, brother and sister, created Marquis a very handsome and sturdy stud cat. He however had a measure of "foreign "blood. Their grandfather Calin des Princes, was a white Persian and their Father Eloi-Eryx, came from another family: the Madalpour family of Mme Chaumont-Doisy.

GB. Then it is not a good idea to mate a brother and sister born in a closely inbred family?

SP. It is better to avoid it as a general rule but one can mate a father with his daughter or mother with her son. It does not have such a negative effect on future generations as is sometimes said.

GB. Close inbreeding, then is not a catastrophe and can show many advantages.

SP. As long as the parents are first rate and their descendants are well bred it is fine. However prolonged inbreeding can diminish the fertility of the cats. That is why it is advisory to supervise the breeding program.

This means choosing a superb male, like Orloff was and mate him to a female from a different family and of a different quality (Nounourse). He was then mated to his daughter (Xenia). Then select the daughters and granddaughters according to their breeding qualities, their sturdiness and their morphology. The same goes for the males and do not keep a scrawny kitten. Although he won't become an international champion, an average cat is still able to be an excellent breeder.

GB. If one looks at the pedigree of Cosima it can be seen that Mlle Boyer worked well and you took over from there. It is also better to understand how breeders you call "merchants," solely preoccupied with the sale value of their cats, bring danger to the breed by putting on the market subjects that carry transmittable defects and they know it.

SP. I had sent out a sort of alarm a few years ago, at the end of 1981, in the newsletter of the Cat Club *La Vie Feline* (the Feline Life). I recommended that all breeders of the sacred cat of Burma be very vigilant in order to keep the breed together. Many cats displayed some defects that I had never personally encountered. They had a white mark on their chin, some white marks climbing up the front paws or some lozenge shaped white marks in their seal or blue markings, or in reverse: dark marks in white gloves. I demanded these cats were retired from breeding.

GB.   Where do you think these defects come from?

SP.   From out crosses with other breeds, badly carried out, over many years, or too many out crosses. It always returns to the problem of selection. If cats with defects are mated, the defects are transmitted and they multiply and develop.

GB.   Jean-Louis de Pindray said on this subject: "I acquired my first female cat, Ophelie in 1965. She did not have a single white mark anywhere on her paws. In actual fact it turned out that one dark lozenge shaped mark appeared on her gloves at around three to four months. More colour loss could be seen on her nose and more white marks on her coat, amongst other places…"

SP.   Alas, researching new colours has caused the breeder to make out crosses which are inevitably not good for the future of the breed.

I am not opposed to the new colours, I am opposed to mixing the breeds and it is not possible to obtain one without the other. Some defects appeared which did not exist at all, or very rarely, when I began my breeding program in1953. I never heard Mlle Boyer say that the first Birmans had visible white markings somewhere on their paws. Not in the original Madalpour or Kaabaa lines.

GB. Basically, applying Mendel's laws on characteristic heredity did not necessarily make the breed better.

SP. Certain foreign breeders, in particular, have used this discovery to create new colours, like they did for the Siamese. Moreover I am not convinced that the Lilac or Cream Birmans was a brilliant idea, since the white gloves are difficult to see on paws that are cream or light pinkish grey.

GB. I met some serious young breeders in France at the Cat Club and the Feline Circle of Paris amongst others who were shocked by the fashion for the Birman in numerous colours. Mlle Dupays owner of Tresor Lune d'Argent, said, " It is a shame as there are already so many difficulties in maintaining the original colour and perfect gloves of the seal point."

SP. She was right and it is worrying. Moreover Jean-Louis de Pindray, had noticed whilst judging Birmans that over the course of five or six years, the tail of the seal point Birman was often tinted blue. This came from mixing blue and seal Birmans to excess. Once again it is necessary to be vigilant.

GB. I read in one of your Newsletters of the Circle, in 1986, a severe warning, demanding that breeders avoid introducing new colours genes into the Birman breed. I quote the text:

"There is much more to do in breeding the cats we currently have (homogeneity of style, gloving, genetic marks, etc.) before considering work on another type. It hardly seems desirable, since the Birman is a gloved cat, to favour the production of pale coloured cats (lilac point) or speckled cats (tortie point) for the obvious reasons of contrast. The "b"genes (necessary for obtaining chocolate points and lilac points) and the "O" orange gene (which gives red points) are all absent in the genetic inheritance of the Birman cat. In order to introduce them, it is necessary to out cross with cats of a different breed and thus put the particular and unique style of the sacred cat of Burma in danger. As things stand at present, the Circle recommends retaining the seal and blue point colourings and to keep "pure" lines by not carrying the genes of colours which are considered undesirable," I found this text interesting and very rational.

GB. Catherine Kreutz, who was a vet, wrote it. She was particularly interested in the genetics of the Birman cat as she had been breeding Birmans since 1979. She worked with me in editing the newsletter of the Circle. I asked her to do this article for me in the name of the Circle. It was very important to me.

GB. I met Dr Kreutz during a Cat Club show. She told me that in Germany they had a breeding committee and that a permit was required to perform a cross between two breeds. In order to obtain this permit, one had to show one's objectives, and the breeding program.

Dr Kreutz said "to create a new variety requires an enormous number of cats because in the first generation the kittens are or can be of intermediary type. One cannot tell the type until the kittens are about two months old. (*Birman kittens are born white. The markings appear clearly on the end of the ears and the end of the nose around two weeks old, at three weeks the gloves are visible but it takes two months before the type can be defined.*)

One therefore needs a strict breeding program for the creation of different coloured varieties?

SP. Inexperienced breeders would do well to give up playing at apprentice sorcerers.

GB. I can imagine Marcelle Baudoin-Crevoisier's reaction! He would be out of his mind with rage!

SP. He was already when I spoke to him about the blue Birman in 1967. Without being reactionary, perhaps he was not completely wrong. He feared the worst! He thought that the sacred cat of Burma, the one the first breeders had shown, especially his Dieu d'Arakan, was the most beautiful cat in the world. "The harmony of his colours, the beauty of his coat and marvellous collar create an almost supernatural animal." He said, "To want to change these characteristics is a crime of treason."

GB.   You agree with him. To seek out new colours so that you can be the first to show an "unpublished" variety and sell it for more, what a risk it is to the breed, what a mistake! Seal or blue the Birman is magnificent the gloves are easily seen especially on the seal Birman. What I love are its "culottes" of fur. It is quite moving to see them from behind, with the dancers' way of walking: one longs to cuddle the silky fur, which asks to be stroked. It ripples under your fingers...

SP.   The famous charm... One cannot resist the Birman cat. Even now I receive letters from people who bought a cat from me ten or fifteen years ago. They send me photographs to show me how they have turned out. Someone even wrote to say their cat had died and they missed it so much that they had replaced it with another sacred cat of Burma. The post I receive is only from France but today the Birman cat is known throughout the world.

CHAPTER 4

THE SACRED CAT OF BURMA ABROAD

Gisele Barnay. Do you enjoy hearing from the people who have written to you, from all over the world, for a long time now, to give you news about cats that you had bred?

Simone Poirier. I love to keep in touch with all Birman cat lovers. In May 1987, I received news about Landri de Crespieres, who went to live in Quebec Canada, twelve years ago. His "mother" Mme Doyer was very emotional as she told me of the death of her seventeen year old cat. Landri was grief stricken and unable to cope with the absence of his old friend. She wanted a new Birman kitten to keep Landri company and I gave her some advice.

GB. It is via North America that the Birman cat

began to conquer the world. The Americans spoke with enthusiasm of the arrival of "Waddi" Irraoudi du Clos Fleuri, the first Birman sent, in 1959, to the home of Dr Seipel in Virginia by Mme Surcel.

SP. Mme Surcel had bought the father of Irraoudi from Mme Chaumont-Doisy. He was Hamlet de Madalpour, the grandson of Yogui de Kaabaa.

Hamlet was also the father of Josika de Clos Fleuri, a blue female sent to America in 1960 and Kairos de Lugh a seal point male also sent to Dr Seipel by Mme Droisier in 1961

GB. In the letters from America which I have read, French Birmans have the reputation of being majestic, very intelligent and prolific. The suffix "Janacques" belonging to Dr and Mme Seipel was applied to fourteen beautiful cats in 1964, the offspring of Josika, Irraouadi, Kairos and Joanne d'Ormailley, who had arrived in 1960.

Hamlet de Madalpour

SP. D'Ormailley was the suffix of Mme Vandalle; Joanne was a cat from her breeding stock. It was at this time that Mrs Griswold came on the scene and I sent Korrigan and Leslie to the United States to her.

GB. In the newsletter Sacred Cat of Burma Fanciers, Mrs Griswold tells the American adventure. Ten years later the sacred cat of Burma had its own club in Ohio. It was possible to learn about the mating of Korrigan of Clover Creek to the "Tibetan" Pkaa Khmer and later of Leslie de La Regnardiere mated to Klaa Khmer. Three beautiful female kittens were born on the 4th June 1963 to Korrigan and Pkaa. Leslie and Klaa produced four kittens one male and three females, born on the 26th August. Mrs Griswold wrote, "We have been very lucky with the number of females."

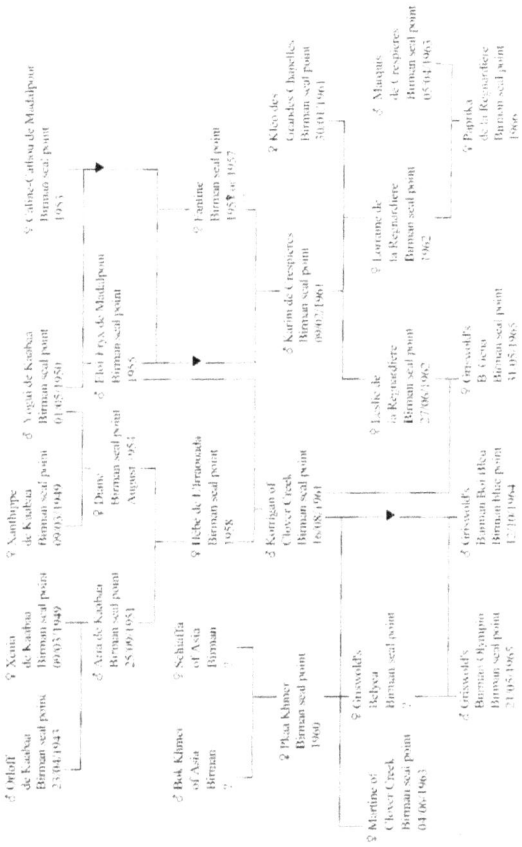

Genealogy of Korrigan and Olympio

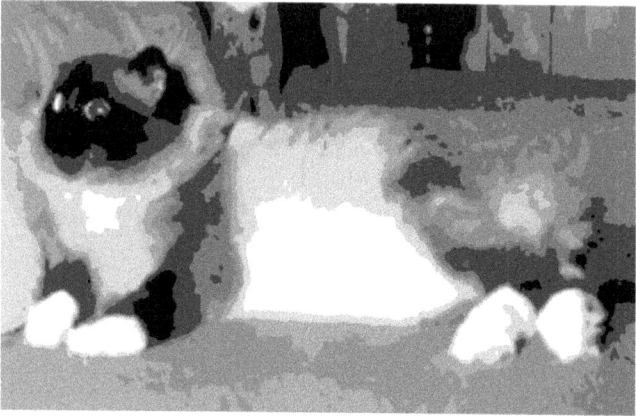

Korrigan of Clover Creek
Korrigan has a deformed ear due to an accident

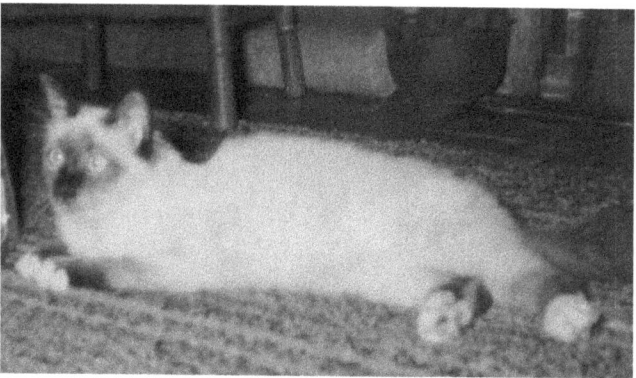

Leslie de la Regnardiere

On the 11th December 1963 she sent you Dablu the son of Leslie and Martine the daughter of Pkaa and Korrigan. I understand that Martine was very afraid after the plane flight.

SP. She was more than afraid: she was traumatised.

We did not have any other way of transporting the cats other than by plane. They left from Seattle Airport, flew over Anchorage in Alaska and landed in London from there another plane took them to Orly. Some coped well with the journey, which took two days back then. Martine did not cope with it at all. She was always very nervous and slightly emotionally disturbed. Despite her superb dark blue eyes, I was never able to show her, as it made her go completely insane.

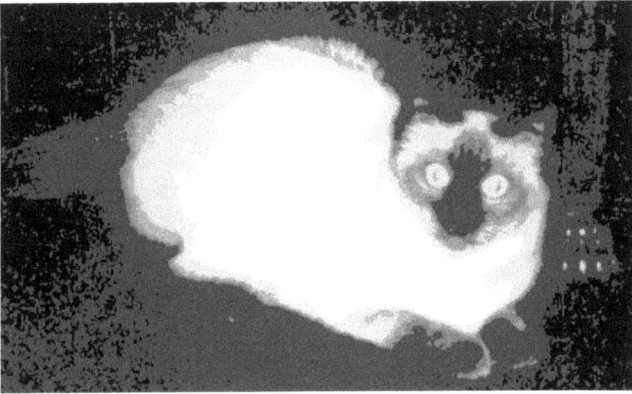

Martine

GB.   How did the kittens travel?

SP.   They travelled in the baggage hold, in comfortable fitted-out Niches. Today, the jets are faster and there are fewer problems but one always runs a certain risk when young cats make the journey alone. It is better for them to be accompanied, and travel in the cabin.

GB. Poor little Martine! What a fright for a six month old kitten to find itself in the baggage hold of a noisy aeroplane. Even if they are nursed and accommodated in the best way possible, it is still hell for sensitive animals.

SP. I also experienced problems when I was sent some kittens from Seattle. In 1965 Olympio arrived in London one Saturday at midday, the hour when everything stops at an airport. I was frantic with worry. I constantly telephoned to find out where my cat was. Luckily when I located him he was not too upset. Mme Griswold and I had agreed that she would send me some products of her breeding program so that I would have another breeding source. That was how Martine, Dablu, Olympio, Gena and Nola came to live in France. I also kept Griswold Burman Boi Bleu for a few months so that he could become a European Champion.

GB. Was he traumatised by the journey?

Griswolds Boi Bleu

SP.   No not at all. Boi Bleu, a superb blue point male, as his name implies, was a year old when he arrived in France in October 1965. He won the title Champion in three shows. At that time it was extremely rare. He made the most of his stay in Europe by taking a trip to Germany to the home of Frau Hackmann. There he mated the international Champion Nadine de Khlaramour. That was the beginning of the blue Birman in Germany.

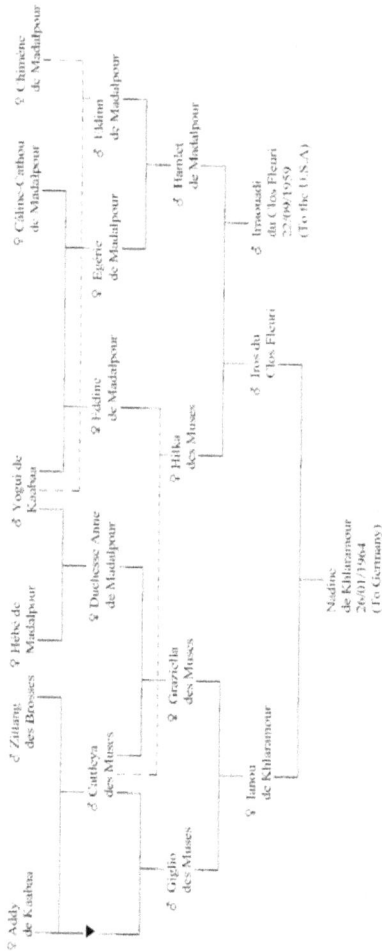

First cats exported to the United States and Germany

GB. What a success! Germany was in its turn conquered by the sacred cat of Burma.

SP. That country, the creator of the Khmer, was not able to remain indifferent when faced with our Birman. The first cat to be imported was Nadine de Khlaramour, who left for the home of Anneliese Hackmann, a passionate breeder. Nadine was the great granddaughter of Hamlet de Madalpour. (Every cat leads back to the Madalpour and Kaabaa lines!) The first kittens were born on the 5th August 1965 they were Ibikus and Iwan von Assindia, two seal points. Now, one comes across a large number of Birmans in Germany, most of them from the von Assindia line.

GB. All you have to do to convince yourself of this is to open at random a cat show catalogue. For example, at the fourteenth Great International Cat Show of Liege, organised by the Cat Club of Brussels 19th March 1969, there were four seal point Birmans from the von Assindia cattery. Xenia, Yvette, Xenio and Kirsten and two blue points: Jugmin and Samka. There is also Gentiana's Sabu, born in May 1967, the son of Or de Crespieres a cat from your breeding program.

SP. Or de Crespieres left for Holland in 1965. He was the son of Martine of Clover Creek and Marquis de Crespieres. I sold Or to Mme van Praag, Gentiana's Sabu who was exported to Holland and shown at Liege, came from M van Praag's cattery.

GENEALOGY OF THE FIRST CATS EXPORTED TO ENGLAND AND HOLLAND

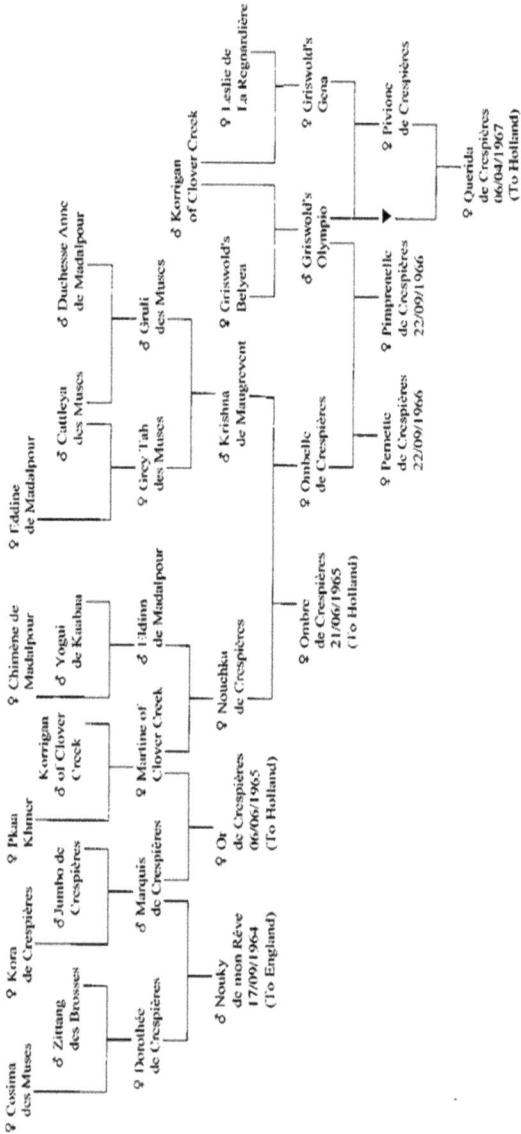

♀ Cosima des Muses

♀ Zittang des Brosses

♀ Kora de Crespières

♂ Jumbo de Crespières

♀ Phau Khmer

♂ Korrigan of Clover Creek

♀ Chimène de Madalpour

♂ Yogui de Kailoua

♀ Eddine de Madalpour

♂ Cattleya des Muses

♀ Duchesse Anne de Madalpour

♂ Domithée de Crespières

♂ Marquis de Crespières

♀ Martine of Clover Creek

♂ Eddinn de Madalpour

♂ Grey Tah des Muses

♂ Gruti des Muses

♂ Korrigan of Clover Creek

♂ Nouky de mon Rêve 17/09/1964 (To England)

♀ Or de Crespières 06/06/1965 (To Holland)

♀ Nouchka de Crespières

♂ Krishna de Maugrevent

♀ Griswold's Belyen

♀ Leslie de La Regrandière

♀ Ombre de Crespières 21/06/1965 (To Holland)

♀ Ombelle de Crespières

♂ Griswold's Olympio

♂ Griswold's Gena

♀ Pernette de Crespières 22/09/1966

♀ Pimprenelle de Crespières 22/09/1966

♀ Pivoine de Crespières

♀ Querida de Crespières 06/04/1967 (To Holland)

first cats Exported to England and Holland

GB. In its turn Holland acquired and developed the breed, I understand there is a Club for the breed in the Low Countries.

SP. It is at Apeldoorn. The same year I sent Or de Crespieres to M van Praag I sent her Ombre. Then I sent Pernette and Pimpernelle de Crespieres, Two daughters of Olympio, to Dr Leeman in 1966. Finally I sent Querida de Crespieres another daughter from Olympio to Mme Jongkamp in 1967.

GB. I have seen that the Dutch cats have had press honours: there is a very good photograph of Or de Crespieres in *Het Parool* an Amsterdam paper, on the 10th December 1966. As I cannot read Dutch I was not able to understand the text. In another paper, one comes across two Birmans belonging to Dr Leeman: their gloves were absolutely perfect. Meanwhile the Americans were becoming more and more involved with the breed.

SP. The CFA (Cat Fanciers Association), the most important cat association in the United States, finally recognised the breed on 1st July 1967. It was a victory. A standard was established, very close to the French one. For a number of years the sacred cat of Burma had been presented in cat shows in the experimental class. Only the seal and blue colourings were recognised. Ten years later, the CFA also recognised the Chocolate and Lilac colourings.

GB. You sent Kora de Crespieres to Mme Griswold. She said that this pretty little cat, a golden eyed completely black cat, had perfect gloves. She was very happy with her pedigree when I met her in 1964. The following year, she reported on the arrival of Opale de Khlaramour: a blue point Birman nine weeks old, sent by Mme Moulin of Nice. The reports sing the praises of the silky fur, the quality of the type, and the beauty of the profound blue gaze, and also the friendly and affectionate nature of the Birman. It was a great success.

SP. The Americans did some good work. My "American" cats were beautiful. For example, Griswold Burman Gena became a champion, in 1969 and an international Champion in 1970, Olympio did too. France has never stopped exporting Birman cats to the United States. Since 1981 Sylphe Bleu du Maoucha was sent to Adrian and Occitane de La Belle Image to Los Angeles along with many others.

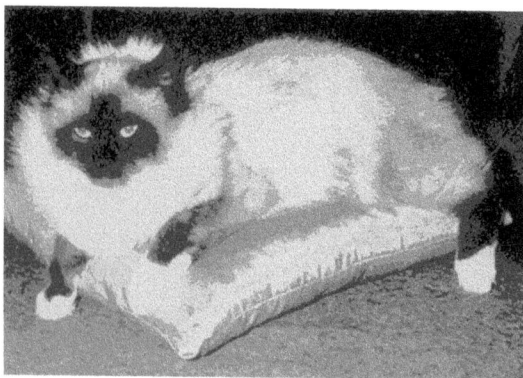

Nouky de Mon Reve

Great Britain became interested in the Birman cat several years after the United States. It was Elsie Fisher a British breeder of Siamese cats who first became fascinated, once she had seen them at a French cat show. She became a Birman enthusiast. Together with Mrs Richards she was one of the first Birman breeders in England. It was I who negotiated the sale of some of the Cat Club's kittens.

Orlamonde de Khlaramour

The first seal point stud cat exported, in 1965, was Nouky de Mon Reve, born in France at the home of Mme Battung. The following year Orlamonde de Khlaramour a blue point female, bred by Mme Moulin was exported. At the same time Mrs Fisher bought another blue female Osaka de Lugh, from Mme Droisier, of the Cat Circle of Paris. These three cats were the start for the Birman breed on the other side of the English Channel.

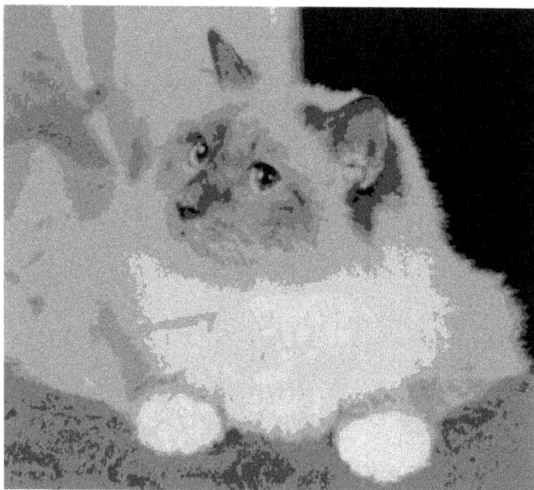

Osaka de Lugh

Pipo du Closs Fleuri

GB. In another article in *The Cat Breeder* in December 1969, Mrs Richards tells how another stud cat Pipo de Clos Fleuri, a cat imported by Mrs Towe in 1967, had contributed to the expansion of the breed. Mrs Fisher explains, in a short open letter to the American Club, how she had been worried about seeing her little female cat Osaka at the end of a long period in Quarantine imposed, by British law, on all imported animals.

SP. With that situation one buys a kitten a few months old and meets it again when it is an adult, ready to breed! Nouky stayed with a vet in Jersey for six months: the legal quarantine period. Imagine the impatience of the breeders. The Birman charmed both Mrs Fisher and Mrs Richards. One described the Birman as the "most intelligent and affectionate" of all cats, and the other hoped that this "Fascinating cat" would come to know the success it deserved in Great Britain.

Praha Hu-Tsung

Anyway if one is to believe Mrs Fisher, the sacred cat of Burma had created its roots. The kittens born in the "Praha" cattery joined those around the world, who came directly from France. Many were exported to Europe and to United States, Canada, Jamaica, New Zealand and Australia.

I have kept the "best Wishes" card Mrs Fisher sent me in 1970. It is a photograph of her International Grand Champion Praha Hu-Tsung, a marvellous seal point. This cat appears in a number of pedigrees throughout the world. He is also a descendant of Yogui de Kaabaa, of Orloff and Fly.

GB.   Mlle Boyer could not have imagined in 1928 that her spoilt kitten at Mourillon would be the starting point of those in Australia! What a great number of descendants!

SP.   Australia is very interested in the Birman. The first pair came from England and were introduced by Judith Starky in 1967. They were Stacpoly Kharma and the female Praha Shigaste, from Mrs Fisher's breeding program. It appears that their popularity grew so fast that other cats had to be swiftly imported from France, England and Germany. At the start seal Points predominated: the blue point arrived a few years later. Some of the pure lines coming from other countries were absolutely necessary for the improvement of the breed. The imports and exports increased the robustness of the kittens.

GB. This mixing of the different lines is actually remarked upon in cat show brochures. One finds an example of this at the end of the Sixties. The English cat Praha Hui Tsu is in Holland at Dr Sengpiel's, and Ghandi von Assindia, a German cat is with Mrs Fisher in England. His brother Guido von Assindia came to France to Mme Moulin's. Krischan von Assindia gave birth in Holland at Mme Jongkamp's, to the kittens of your Querida de Crespieres. Qui-ly Khan de Ranchipur, a French cat, partnered Iris Von Assindia in Germany and one of their kittens Solomon Von Assindia went to live in Great Britain where he became a grand champion! It is all very amusing.

Solomon Von Assindia (Photo by Ann Cumbers)

SP. It is a better way of limiting the risks of inbreeding.

Today there are many sacred cats of Burma and breeders are able to choose their stud cats. They no longer come up against the difficulties that confronted us after the war and up until 1953.

GB.   The sacred cat of Burma has come a long way, in the sixty years since its first appearance at the cat show of 1926. It is quite extraordinary that the cat is now found From New Zealand to Scandinavia, passing through Denmark and Luxembourg on the way.

SP.   The cat has truly conquered Northern Europe. One Swedish breeder Marie Persson, has become a member of my French Circle and we have her to thank for the fact that in Sweden around four hundred Birman kittens are born each year. It is amazing how popular the breed is there.

GB.   The first export to Sweden was Riki de Ranchipur bought in 1968 from Mme Boning of the Chinospins cattery. It was a cat from the breeding program of Jean-Louis de Pindray. I read in your newsletter of the Circle that the first litter was born at the home of M. Hogberg, at the Silverbacken cattery. Seventy Swedish breeders have registered their suffices.

European Premier & European Champion
Arbaybi Bashful Beau 1982-2000

SP.   Sweden also has its own Birman Cat Club: it can be said that the breed has met with enormous success there. The Club has been in existence since 1977 and has around five hundred members. Marie Persson reports that on average about sixty cats take part in each show (thirty seal, thirty blue) and that their country has very beautiful champions, such as Arbaybi Bashful Beau, who came from Great Britain.

GB.   Jean-Louis de Pindray, who often went to Sweden to judge the Birmans, told me that their blue points were particularly magnificent. There they have the same proportion of cats with good gloves as we do in France, which is said to be about 40%. The Swedes have a type of quarantine, like the British, except the cats are only isolated for four months. This brought a few problems of inevitable inbreeding, as you experienced at the beginning of your breeding program.

SP. I know, due to this quarantine rule, which is very contentious, there is very little interest in importing.

Marie Persson confirmed that the regularity and symmetry of the gloves was difficult to set, as it was in France... and everywhere, it is hardly surprising. The researchers, such as M. Dreux, who were interviewed on the subject of "colouring" many years ago, said that the function and nature of the responsible genes were not well known. How childish it was that some of the novice breeders thought they had dealt with the problem and I find it dangerous that they only care about obtaining the new colours. The Swedes, who work in a closed circuit, are proof that we must be prudent.

GB. It is obvious. All the countries of the world have the same percentage of well-gloved Birmans, pure Birmans. Since, then they have introduced some cats whose pedigree is riddled with all colours of Siamese or colour points. The reasoning is warped it is up to each breeder to give it their attention, from the Antipodes to Alaska!

SP.   I do not think that one would find many Birmans in Alaska-except in the planes which fly over Anchorage-but there are some in Norway and Finland.

GB.   There are even some in the Far East. I read in the Cat Club magazine, *La Vie Feline* that one was sent to Singapore in 1974. Perhaps if he was allowed to go out, he met his Siamese cousins of the streets… but Jaipur de Ranchipur would not lose his way with a gutter- urchin, even an Asian one, he no longer had any physical resemblance to him.

SP.   Fly de Kaabaa would no longer recognise his descendants. These luxury cats have also been bred in Japan, including one seal point female born in 1979 at the home of M Tumagai in Tokorosawa. I discovered that she even had a slightly Japanese name, Orchidee de la Maison Bleue.

GB.   In our tour of the world I had forgotten South Africa.

SP.   The first sacred cat of Burma to arrive there was Thimothy de Ranchipur, the son of Sinh Francis de Mun-Ha and Princesse de Ranchipur. He went to Montevideo in Uruguay in 1970. Since then there have certainly been many others. Of those exported from the Cat Club, I can only recall Valerie de Ranchipur and Vladimir de Koster sent to Brazil in 1972 and 1973.

GB.   What journeys and what conquests. There have

been some in Africa for a few years in Cameroon and
Senegal: Robinson and Sari de la Belle Image. Nothing
can stop the Birman. I hope the new masters make
sure the journey is in the cabin, so that the ordeal that
Martine experienced can be avoided. It is much easier
for a Birman puss to colonise Belgium.

SP. Belgium was certainly not deprived, as we saw a
long time ago they had amongst other conquerors, the
beautiful Lon Saito of Mlle Rousselle in 1933 and the
pretty Zaquelle de Mandalay. Unfortunately like so
many others they did not survive the war. The breeders
had to start from scratch again.

GB. I noticed in the diaries of Mlle Boyer a little note
at the bottom of a page: Xylou de Kaabaa departed for
Brussels in May 1950 to the home of Mme Walton-
Delmotte. Another Kaabaa to breed in Belgium, it is
about time he made kittens.

SP. Moreover they mated with some new lines; the
Belgians are very interested in the sacred cat of Burma.
Many Birmans that I know have been sent to Belgium,
including Sphinx Bleu du Maoucha and Scarlett de La
Belle Image. More recently Basilic Bleu Nui de Maoucha
went to the home of M.Antoine, the president of the
Belgian Birman Cat Club in Kraainem. Basilic was
born on 28th April 1986.

GB. I am astonished that the Belgians had not created

THE SECRETS OF THE SACRED CAT OF BURMA

their own Birman Cat Club earlier, since they were amongst the first to breed Birmans.

SP. They decided too and the club became official in June 1987. It was a good thing, since it was well known that they had been very keen about cat breeding and in particular the Birman since the twenties and thirties.

GB. Switzerland is no more of a risk than Belgium when it comes to transporting kittens. The Swiss, including Abbot Chamonin, are amongst the greatest "Birmanophiles," one might say.

SP. That description fits the Abbot well; he always loved and defended the Birman cat.

GB. M. Mannes, an international Judge with FIFe, told me that after the war there were very few Birman cats remaining in Switzerland "The main breeding sources were the ones in France." he said, " In 1954 Mme Hedy Troendle, of Zurich, bred the descendants of Andaman de Karabula and Civah de Madalpour. Some from the Khlaramour line can also be found."

SP. Ulyssia de Ruvelisaya, the daughter of Grand Champion of Europe Sheridan du Ruvelisya, went to Geneva in 1983. During the course of thirty years, Swiss breeding had been perfectly restructured and a huge number of Birmans had been imported.

GB. One dip into the catalogue of the Feline

Association of France Parisian cat show of January 1965 shows that Mme Trussel, who came from Switzerland, had shown four female cats: Moussia, Krisis, Mousmee de Khlaramour and Natouschy and a male cat Nebolio de Birkenof. One also finds, between 1974 and 1986, the names of Iang de Ranchipur at Neuchatel, Maharani and Sissi des Monts Naga at Lausanne, Phelicite de La Belle Image at Bienne, Tony de La Belle Image and Bunji de Ruvelisaya at Geneva…and that is just a sample. The Swiss, like the Belgians, are very close neighbours to us and they take part in most of the French cat Shows.

SP.   In the same way that France takes part in the Swiss and Belgian shows. As you have said they are close neighbours and the journey is not a long one for the kittens and the champions.

GB.   We will soon be reaching our limit. Amongst all the named cats and the countries in which they have been paraded, the Spanish accent has rarely come up.

SP.   Perhaps although two of my cats went to Spain, they did go to a Dutch couple M. and Mme van Praag, to whom I sold Or and Ombre de Crespieres. The name of their cattery Gentiana's sounds a little Spanish.

M. and Mme van Praag lived in Valencia for a few years and wanted to sell their stock when they were too old to continue to take care of them. They wrote to me asking me to help them to home the cats which remained with them, making it clear that the Spanish were hardly interested in the cats of this breed. There was a Spanish Feline Association, a member of the International Federation but it is possible, that exported Birmans, (for example Irene des Monts Naga, a blue point who went to live in Madrid in 1975) dwelt more often with expatriates, like M. and Mme van Praag, rather than native Spaniards. I have not really studied the situation.

GB.   There remains one country of Latin culture that gave us much to dream about in our journey researching the Birman: it is Italy. She remains the adoptive country of Dieu de d'Arakan and Regina de Rangoon, who left this world with few remaining traces.

SP.   It's a bit of a shame; Dieu d'Arakan could have been like Yogui, the grandfather of thousands of sacred cats of Burma. It was enough for him to be beautiful.

GB.   He and Reine de Rangoon do not to our knowledge, have any descendants in Italy. That has not prevented the Italians from fervently defending the Birman.

SP.   He is very well loved in Italy, where Franca Gabriele created his club in Turin.

GB.   The very name of this club is a listing in itself: *Associazione Italiana Amatori del Gatto Sacro di Birmania.* One longs to sing it! Dieu d'Arakan finally happened to meet his death in Italy. He had better things to do than procreate: a big star, he departed in the prime of life in the country of sun and of *bel canto*. He was replaced with many other cats that came from France.

SP. There were a great number, over the years, which crossed the border. I received an invitation to the first "Birman special," organised in Turin on the 12th and 13th November 1983. It was the forty-second Italian International Cat Show. It was predominantly a celebration of the sacred cat of Burma.

Eu Ch Attila des Chouettes Sages

GB. There is no more to say, as one could not list the names of the all the French Birmans sent to Italy. It would be better to go and admire them in a *Esposizione Felina*.

Interestingly, many Birmans originating from the cattery

de La Belle Image are in Turin, Genoa, Milan and so on. There followed Siphorel de la Renouee, sent to the home of Mme Nuoletta in 1981. They have preceded a number of others, including Attila des Chouettes Sages, who went to the home of Mme Gabriele. The Italians love the Birman because they love beauty.

SP.   There is not a country where the Birman cat is not admired for its character, its look, and its fur…

GB.   Mrs Richards, in an article, compared the fur of the sacred cat of Burma to swan's down, light and misty. In all continents he is loved for his discreet presence, his sweet voice, his pleasant bearing, his intelligence. All those things which seduced me.

SP.   When I hear you talk about Onyx, I envy you. I always had O'lise-Lison my lovely Burmese but since the death of Semele, I confess that I have missed the sacred cat of Burma. He is such an endearing creature… I can understand the people who have written to me saying that their cat has died and left a great void in their lives.

CHAPTER 5

✿

ON PERSONALITY
AND CHARACTER

Gisele Barnay. In thirty years of breeding, you have seen the birth of numerous cats; you must have some good memories.

Simone Poirier. I have forgotten the number and names of all the cats that I have bred. I have not worked as you would in a factory, counting my pieces of work. The kittens were sold at three months old and I have very patchy memories of them. As for my cats, I have a huge amount of affection for them. Cosima, Dorothee, Folie, Fantine, Martine, Ines, and Semele I cannot forget them, no more than I could Olympio, the only male amongst a thousand girls!

GB. With all those kittens born at your home, your

memories must be like those of an actual midwife and you must have plenty of stories.

SP.   For a long time, I birthed the cats of my friends and the friends of my friends. They would come to collect me, or telephone me in the middle of the night, for a birth in Paris. I would call a taxi and depart immediately. Luxury cats have many whims; they often refuse the lined basket prepared for them. They prefer to go and lie in a bed, a wardrobe or the drawer in a chest of drawers. If they are moved and put in their basket, they return to the place they have chosen and it is pointless to try to reason with them. The birth will take place there and not where you decided it would.

GB.   You have told us how Plume de Crespieres, the cat of Marc Doelnitz, would only lie in a drawer where he had arranged his boas from Marabou. That's typically eccentric for the cat of an artist.

SP.   It was a pretty sight, the little white pompons on the multicoloured feathers. At the home of my friend Mme Lemoine, her Birman had made a less poetic decision: to lie beneath the pile of dusters neatly arranged in her wardrobe. As the pile of dusters was on the first shelf, it was necessary to kneel throughout the birth.

GB.   What about yours? What were their foibles?

SP. Mine preferred to lie in my bed! There they felt completely secure. It was a marvellous display of their trust but not very practical. Anyway, a Birman always comes to find you before going into labour. She makes you understand that she needs you.

GB. Francine de Pindray told me the story about the birth of some of Princesse's Kittens and it was very touching. The cat stayed near her so that she would be sure the birth would go well.

SP. That does not surprise me. Fantine waited for me on the day of a cat show. She was in her basket, where she wanted to stay. The veterinary surgeon had been to my house twice because I was concerned. A cat cannot be alone at the end of her gestation period. I returned as quickly as I could. Fantine gave birth to her first kitten as soon as I was near her.

GB. Is a cat able to put off her contractions for a whole day?

SP. Probably, in any case I noticed it particularly on that occasion as well as at other times. Fantine waited for me for a number of hours. When one of my cats was on the verge of giving birth, she would follow me everywhere. The presence of a loved master is very important for a Birman. There is no such relationship with farm cats; they hide their newly born in a hayloft because they are forbidden to enter into the house.

GB.   It's a world of difference, but common cats are excellent mothers and want to protect their little ones.

SP.   Birmans cats are also good mothers. It is easy to get them to adopt orphaned kittens. Obviously one must completely trust the owner, to ensure you don't come across the same problems I had when my cats got ringworm because of an underhand breeder.

GB.   Have you tried it on other occasions?

SP.   Yes, with a friend of Mme Ravel who I knew well. Her Persian had a caesarean. Asleep she could not feed her three newly born kittens. I brought Folie along, who had some kittens fifteen days old. I placed her on the bed and gently stroked her and then we put the three Persian kittens next to her. She accepted them completely and groomed them. They suckled from her for no less than two hours, greedily, because they were hungry. During that time the anaesthetised Persian gradually came back to life. When she was able to look after the little ones, Folie returned to her own kittens as if nothing had happened. In another serious situation, when alas, the mother had died, a friend brought her kittens to my house and one of my cats raised them with her own litter.

GB.   That doesn't happen whilst they are in the bottom of a wardrobe?

SP.   No, once the little ones are born and they have

suckled, one can easily move them into a basket or breeding pen. It is essential that the place is "reassuring" to use a modern expression. Having said that, there are some terrible cats who drag their offspring around the whole apartment.

GB. If you have other cats, wouldn't they pick up the kittens of the others…?

SP. My cats looked after their kittens together. The kittens did not mind which mother they suckled, and the litters became intermingled. It was difficult to find where they were! Moreover I have noticed that the social bearing of cats that have lived, happily, in a community is very different to those left to their own devices.

GB. They organise their own society and establish their own hierarchy. There must have been less jealousy amongst twenty cats than between two or three in one house.

SP. Certainly and when a kitten had an accident they all rallied round. Thyra's experience is a good example of this. At the age of three months whilst playing she fell from the fifth story to the lawn. I couldn't find her I looked everywhere. The next morning, I made enquiries with my neighbours. A neighbour on the ground floor had found her in front of her door, instead of informing someone and trying to find the owner, the kitten was put in the cellar on a rag.

Thyra was cold and wet. It had rained the previous evening and she was shaking and her fur was all wet. We put her in a big basket with woollens and warm towels. Thank God she had not broken anything. The vet diagnosed only serious trauma. A Miracle! But she continued shaking. The most astonishing thing was the attitude of the other cats: the adult cats including big Olympio who was very careful not to hurt her, positioned themselves around and on top of Thyra to warm her up. I was able to sleep well; the community restored Thyra. The more numerous the cats, the better they get along with each other. The rules of their hierarchy are quietly established and Thyra was a baby they had to protect.

GB. It was marvellous and very important because a bad experience can upset a cat for the rest of its life. The Birman is sensitive enough to remember the better and worse events. Martine never forgot her plane trip.

SP. I told you that although she was a ravishing cat, she could not bear to go to cat shows. She lived in my studio in "Rue Saint-Ferdinand" and she gradually took the risk of going down to the gallery but she remained afraid. It was necessary to give her constant care and attention. Affectionate and adorable she had an extraordinary look about her. I could not stay with her day and night; I occasionally went away on holiday.

GB. How did you manage that?

SP.   When I had many cats, I only went away for about ten days and my friend Mme Vandalle came to "cat sit." Bizarrely, Martine, who knew Mme Vandalle very well and was not afraid of her, after my departure she inched herself under the stairs as far as the hatch that gave access to the bathroom pipe work. She stayed under the bath for the ten days: nothing would make her come out. Mme Vandalle became desperate; she tried tempting her with morsels of her favourite food, but without success.

When I returned Martine had not eaten for over a week. I called out to the four paws in front of the hatch: "what are you doing under there, Martine?" She came out immediately. I had many big hugs and she devoured her food but from that day, she has obstinately refused to come down to the gallery.

GB.   Perhaps during her plane trip she had a traumatic incident with one of the employees in charge of the animals' needs? Her reaction when faced with your friend cannot be explained any other way, since she was sociable with cats. But she only trusted you.

SP.   It's possible. I spoke to her like I did to my other cats, without raising my voice and as gently as possible. I talk to them in the same way that I talk to my plants. Martine was a delicate plant. She died at the age of three, whilst giving birth to three stillborn kittens.

GB. Even when a cat is perfectly mentally balanced, a cat is sensitive to voices. Onyx, my "only" cat, reacted to the slightest of intonations. The famous intelligence of the Birman cat is, I think, above all due to his extreme sensitivity. Speech does not disturb the cat if he believes he is understood and loved.

SP. It's the golden rule for teaching cats in general and the Birman in particular. It is enough to understand that and never force anything. Each individual expresses himself differently, according to his personality, which regularly asserts itself. My neighbour across the landing always spoke of Yann de Crespieres, one of my three months old kittens. I had accused him of having a wee to the side of his tray and scolded him. One day, he had a wee rather pointedly, in front of the neighbour, scratching his litter and meowing to get attention. The true culprit was Sonia, an adult who was jealous of the little one. I was determined to catch her in the act so that I could restore order. It was a wasted effort there were no further recurrences and when the kitten left the adult cats settled their differences amongst themselves.

GB. I noticed this also, when Onyx lived with Vichnou, my Chartreux cat: as soon as he arrived in the house at three months old, he dominated the Chartreux cat who was six years old. Vichnou was a darling of a cat and never let anyone dominate him except Onyx. There's no denying he had a way about him! Extremely cuddly, Onyx had a seductive authority!

SP.   It's all down to the character of the sacred cat of Burma. Semele bore herself like a foreign princess. When she lived with other cats, both Birman and Burmese, she ignored them, keeping her distance. Later, she only lived with Ines de Pagan and O'Lise, who got on well, whilst she maintained the same dominant bearing. O'Lise for example would not go into my daughter's bedroom where Semele slept but after Semele died she gradually asserted herself. We noticed her progress day by day, everything happened in an unobtrusive way. The hierarchy that existed between the two sacred cats of Burma slightly excluded O'Lise from their world. Today, O'Lise has worked her way into my daughter's bedroom and installed herself onto her bed.

GB.   Francine de Pindray had both Birmans and Burmese also noticed the same behaviour. There were quite a few debates about precedence! Loa-Tsun, the Birman cat would not fight; he held his head up high, very aloof and that was that. He remained dignified when the other cat wanted a fight! The haughty character of the Birman has come perhaps to receive the admiration it demands: he knows he is beautiful. Perhaps Onyx had a rather undignified way off rolling himself around on the carpet with the grace of a kitten to demonstrate his love. His dignity showed itself with my other cats more then with me. His attitude was the evidence of his love, an extraordinary sign of trust. Such quality cuddles, such charm, when we awoke in the morning! He nibbled at my hand and put his little cold nose in my neck he purred and snuggled up next to me, just like a baby seeking contact with its mother.

SP.   Even the grandest champion lets himself go in his displays of affection. It is completely different with a dog, which constantly expresses his feelings publicly. The most affectionate and the cuddliest of cats reserves his true show of affection for when he is alone with his master. He is discreet.

GB.   Although like a child, a cat is never childish. He is always serious and important. It is undoubtedly for those reasons that he holds such a position.

SP.   That is why I miss Ines and Semele, Ines was the baby. Very cuddly she would soon come onto your knee and whenever passing by, she would look for an affectionate word or gesture. Queen Semele, the more beautiful of the two, let herself go when we were alone, like Onyx did with you. We lost her after seventeen years together: it was a bit like losing a child…

It is a loss of beauty as much as a way of life. Look at the blue eyes of Onyx, his light fur, swaying gait and consider his wisdom, it is so enriching. The cat is blessed with happiness; his pleasures do not bring him either illness or neuroses. Only man is able to harm or destroy him. The cat stops eating when he is no longer hungry. He will lie in the sun until the rays are too hot, he then moves into the shade, stretches and splays, showing his stomach all calm and protected. Or he might equally go and sit on top of a pile of papers, on the desk where his mistress writes. Onyx is very blessed but I hope to keep him a while longer as a paperweight, even though he slightly impedes the progress of my work.

SP.   Ah! How a cat loves to sit on papers! They are skilled at positioning themselves right in the middle of the letter you are writing.

GB.   Onyx told me what to write! He put his nose on the page and his grey-blue paws with white gloves played with the pen I held. I might push him gently to the left, onto a heap of papers and write to the right, slightly cramped and at an angle. I have to give up! The only way to send him off without being cruel is to give him a big "head" cuddle, with my hair gently tickling him. He then shakes and licks himself, shoots me a sidelong look of criticism for my bad manners and then calmly spreads himself out on his preferred couch.

SP.   Cats have an innate sense of comfort and Birmans have this from their infancy. To sleep and wake on cushions is one of their principal occupations.

GB.   Yes, and a worried cat never shows its stomach while he sleeps. He crouches, his ears pricked up and he lies dormant although he is not utterly asleep. Onyx stretches and rolls himself up like a snail. He has a personal way of making his bed. I put a big bath towel on "his" sofa so that he doesn't cover it with white hairs. That doesn't please him. He rolls the towel into a ball, pushes away the cushions and curls up in the space he has made. He always makes a nest. In the country, he sleeps under a baby's cotton quilt, although I place him on the top, and very rarely underneath and it's the same throughout the summer. He loves to have a roof over his head and it is very funny to see him do it and I need to brush the sofa afterwards!

SP.   This behaviour is very characteristic of a cat at a show. Many cats hide themselves beneath the lining of their cage. It is tiresome for them to remain enclosed for between 10 and 18 hrs over the course of two days.

GB.   A cat when mobile it is an entirely different situation. For Onyx, it is almost a game of hide-and-seek. When someone he doesn't know knocks at the door. (He recognises the sounds of regular visitors), He hides under the cloth which covers a low table in the lounge or the covered round table in my bedroom. There, he knows that no one will mess him around, like cats at the shows. They become upset because they hate to be enclosed and the people who march up and tickle them, annoy them. I don't mind that Onyx won't be a champion. He is beautiful to me, for breeding stock, there is another point of view. It is important for kittens to have a handsome pedigree and normal for a star to have obligations but I am not sure what the star think of it…

SP. Generally they hate being closely scrutinised. Many hide themselves under the linings or turn their backs on the public. There are some exceptions certain pedigreed cats including Birmans are show-offs. They strike a pose and are used to being admired. Folie loved being stroked and she enjoyed cat shows. In fact it was sometimes necessary to push her to the back of the cage so that visitors could not play with her.

There is much training and preparation for a cat show. There are the logistics, if a cat is forbidden to get on the table in your house, he will refuse to get on the table where he is to be examined by the judge. I have seen this situation for three or four months one has to make the cat accustomed to being handled in this way at the show. They need to be put on a table, have their teeth looked at, be brushed, combed, this needs to be done gently and regularly also before a show they need to have a bath.

GB. There is also the journey. This time the cats are accompanied but again they need to be used to it.

SP. Cats should always be transported in their carrying boxes as it is dangerous for them and the driver if they were loose and happened to panic. They stay calm in their small individual carrier on their usual blanket. When I travelled on a sleeper train, my cats came to sleep with me. There was no danger since the compartment door and the door to the corridor were closed. The movement of the train soothed them. For a long journey, the night train was a good solution. The next morning the cats were fresh and in good form.

GB.   When I took Onyx away for a weekend or on holiday, I always took the same taxi to the station. The driver knew us and accepted that my boy would settle himself on the back shelf. I kept an eye on him throughout the journey and I stroked and cuddled him if he became afraid in a tunnel. He had a fear of tunnels. On a train he remained in his box, relatively well behaved.

What a joy it was to arrive! He took possession of the Bourgogne house, sniffing almost everything. First priority: a wee in the tray that is permanently left in an accessible place. After a light snooze the exploration of the courtyard and garden.

It is not wise to let a town cat out in the country immediately, even if he knows the place well.

SP.   Except for the time when I had too many cats, mine always came on holiday with me. We stayed for a month, sometimes in a hotel in Brittany, sometimes at friend's houses in Collioure or in the country in Moret near Fontainebleu.

GB.   Did you have any problems at the hotel?

SP.   I never had any problems with hotel owners. Ines,

Semele and Lison each travelled in their own carrying case. I let them out in the bedroom once they were used to it. Arlette and I taught them to walk on a lead and we went for walks on the beach. One day a lady appeared with two Scottie dogs running free. They went for our cats. Terrified Semele Ines and Lison attached themselves to us and climbed up into our arms. We had very bloodied hands! The lady out for a stroll had caused us a fair amount of injury. It was the last straw!

GB. The moral is to always keep an eye out for rude holidaymakers who act as though they own the place.

SP. After that incident, the cats refused to go out…we dared not take them for any more walks. At our friends homes they go out with or without a lead while they are watched. At Collioure, Ines is at home and she knows all the routes. She acts like a perfectly common cat, enticed by the smells, the slightest rustling of the grass, the flight of insects or the swift passage of a lizard…

GB. To sense, scratch, hunt and play it's all in the feline nature. It is one of the joys of the summer. At Versailles, in spite of his "aristocratic" pedigree, Onyx races along the neighbourhood paths, without harm, at five o'clock in the morning. Sometimes I go with him. The blackbirds are just starting to sing, as the sun rouses itself. It wakens the scents of all the plants. Nepenthe and mint, carnation and lavender entice him. Spruce, pine and juniper send him into a trance. He sniffs the earth, rubs himself against a tree trunk, smells a trailing branch for a long while and rolls himself on the carpet of pine needles, visibly drunk on conifer fumes. In the country he rediscovers some hazy memories of strong scents, resinous ones, which bother him. He is castrated but that did not prevent him marking his territory a wee here, a wee there at the corner of a wall or the base of a shrub. He only makes a few marks he is economical. If he meets another cat, it all depends…either he knows the cat and greets it, or he runs away. If he hears a dog he runs for it, I watch him retreat at top speed. He does not wait for a confrontation. He has bad memories of an incident with a Boxer…

SP.   With certain dogs, Folie and Ines were all cheek. I took Folie to the home of a breeder M. Le Tallec, who had a Birman stud cat and two Chow dogs. They lived in part of the dining room, separated off by a little device, thirty centimetres high, which they could not jump over. Folie leaped over the obstacle and went to see the chows. At Collioure, Ines passed in front of a neighbour's dogs without concern. They did not bark they seemed staggered by her authority.

GB.   When dogs don't run or bark cats are less bothered about them. Your cats came to realise that the Chows and the dogs at Collioure were harmless. If they are not afraid they surrender themselves to the sensual delights of summer.

SP. At Moret, near our friends house there was a tame magpie. It sometimes came to visit us; the fascinated cats snapped their teeth together with desire. Pinned to the ground, they watched the bird intently. Trying to catch it, they discovered hunting, their instincts came to the fore...

GB. All their senses are awakened in that blessed season where each moment seems planned for the happiness of the cats, sacred or not. Look at them: Semele fascinated by the magpie when it flies off, Ines hunting a butterfly in the meadow before it has been mowed. Onyx lying in wait for a grasshopper. The air is charged with animal and vegetable smells that rouse one or other of them. The midday heat favours sleeping with the sacred hour of rest. The scene changes: Lascivious cats sleep in the shade, other cats take a spot of sunshine on the warm paving slabs of the patio. Cats, half-curled up on a sandy path savouring the freshness of the evening. The soft fur of our Birmans is sensitive to hot hay or fresh grass. They are magnificent amongst tamed nature. Let us leave them whilst they free their ancestral instincts a little. They love us more when we understand them, but do they realise how well we know them...

SP. This type of sixth sense, which means they are aware of our arrival well before the key is in the lock, always intrigued me. In the apartment, my cats knew the sound of someone coming up the stairs and did not bother to move if it was a neighbour coming up. When it was Arlette who was ascending the stairs, they ran as a single group towards the door and waited for her. How did they know it would be her? They had grouped themselves together before they could have detected the sound of her ascending the stairs. Could they recognise her step from the other side of the building? I swear I have never understood it.

GB. Love has an antennae and the sacred cat of Burma has inexplicable intuition and spontaneous enthusiasm, more than other breeds.

SP. Their own stories of love are mysterious. I'll tell you about the love of Olympio and Ophelie. When Jean- Louis de Pindray brought me his first queen to mate to Olympio, Olympio was one year old. What happens is that the young lady moves off and he meets her, with nothing happening, of course. The queen is on the defensive. She strikes out at the male. This is the beginning of the feline ritual. At first flirtatious and aggressive, the queen only allows herself to be seduced after several hours have elapsed. With Ophilie and Olympio it was love at first sight. My beautiful "American" tomcat was ecstatic with his Fiancée. She accepted him immediately. We left them together and they slept with their paws intertwined, they adored each other.

GB. Jean-Louis de Pindray told me that Ophelie had no other partner than Olympio.

SP. Their love story was exemplary. Each time Ophelie came to see him, they recognised each other in the blink of an eye, they sniffed each other and exchanged cat-kisses, by touching noses. They would then wrap themselves around each other. Their first kitten could only be a little marvel: Princesse, who Francine will tell you about in chapter six.

GB. Princesse was a child of love, beautiful, intelligent, and expressive beyond words according to her breeders, who told me another pretty love story about Jessy.

SP. Instinct, sixth sense...the cat is an inigma. We have made much progress in the research of the sacred cat of Burma and we could talk about him for a thousand and one nights, like the Persian stories of the same name.

GB. Does he need a legend? I have asked you and other specialists, many questions. From geneticists to historian, from geographer to zoologist, we have had a tour of this marvellous cat. We have lived, and we continue to live, with him. The further we advance in the knowledge of his proud little soul, the more we realise the impenetrable mystery within.

CHAPTER 6

THE STORY OF PRINCESSE

In the portrait gallery of celebrated Birmans, Princess de Ranchipur occupies a privileged spot: this international champion is still in all the papers of the Cat Club. She was the daughter of Ophelie de Pouh-Miloh, the first female cat of Jean-Louis de Pindray, and the famous Olympio of Simone Poirier, born at the home of Mrs Griswold in Tacoma, Washington in the United States. In December 1966 at four months old Princesse, their love child, was awarded "Best Kitten" and "Excellent First" in a cat show in Amsterdam. Less than a year later, at the Parisian Cat Show in October 1967, she began her career as a star. She had already become a mother and had a painful memory of it…

Princesse's first labour was quite difficult. The contractions of her uterus were long and painful, one after the other. The kittens were in the breech position. "I helped the little ones into the world with infinite care." Relates, Francine de Pindray, "Those terrible contractions, the piercing meows, the big eyes with dilated pupils, told me all the sufferings and agonies of the little mother Princesse." Three hours later, four white blobs cried out from between the paws of their mother and four greedy mouths found swollen nipples of a Princesse finally happy and purring.

One year later, the beautiful Birman, a champion already, came to the end of her second gestation. "I was busy in the kitchen one morning," said Francine, "when Princesse came along, circling me, meowing insistently, coming and going more and more frequently between my feet and the door, coming, going and meowing more and more strongly. I stopped what I was doing and went towards her, but she went off, still meowing, towards the bedroom, where she leapt on to our bed. There, she lay on her side and I gently stroked her tummy. Then she rolled onto her back, with her paws in the air, so that I could gently massage her nipples and calm her down"

It was impossible for Francine to return to her chores as mistress of the house. "as soon as my hand made a slight retreat, Princesse's two front paws grabbed my wrist and she began to meow again and I thought I felt a spasm underneath my hand. The cat seemed to be saying to me "I need you!" I stroked her painful stomach anew and she calmed down. All day as I was going to leave her, because I had two young children Princesse's paws held onto my hand with incredible strength. She jumped down from the bed, followed me every step, meowing tragically and thus always succeeding in drawing me back to the bedroom."

The following night she carried on in the same way. Francine's hand had to stay on the stomach of the Birman, who would not leave her alone. The next day was also identical. At the end of the second night, five kittens came into the world, without a hint of drama. "I realised," said Francine, "that Princesse had not forgotten her first pregnancy when she had been in distress. She put on a perfect act for the two days and I had been caught in the trap, believing each time, in the face of her tricks, that she was going to give birth immediately."

What an amazing memory cats have: they rarely forget painful events in their lives. The moving sensitivity of the Birman wanting no more suffering, turning with trust to those who will not let her down. "For all Pricesse's nine labours, the same scenario unfolded. I was less concerned but I always played the game and reassured her with kind words and gestures."

THE STORY OF JESSY

Jessy was an adorable Birman born to Francine and Jean-Louis Pindray on 21st June 1974. Her mother, the Birman Vicky de Pagan, was not tired as she had only given birth to two little kittens. At two and a half months old, Jessy found some kind parents in Clamart, on the outskirts of Paris. Immediately they took her away on holiday with them. They went to the country, into a single story house overlooking a garden, where it was pretty good to caper about. She was watched over as she played because she was only a kitten; she spent a joyous summer there. The return home was tragic. In the turmoil of returning, Jessy's new parents did not realise that a young kitten does not know danger but has already acquired some bad habits. To jump from a widow at garden level onto the lawn, was a game. At Clamart, Jessy wanted to continue her fun and exploration, someone had accidentally left the window open and she jumped out. This window was on the second floor. At three months old, when a kitten makes a jump in complete confidence, it does not necessarily land on its feet.

"We had just come back from our own holidays," said Jean-Louis, "when Jessy's owners anticipating our return, arrived at our house in a wild panic, with their poor smashed up kitten, begging us to help them," The vet immediately treated and bandaged her. She had suffered a serious fracture of the hip. She was very weak and had to rest completely, without moving. What a problem! "We placed her on a cellulose mattress. She relieved herself like a baby and she had to be cleaned up without causing her any harm. She was kept alive by intramuscular injections of Plasma of Quinton, twice a day for three weeks. She was fed by hand, like a bird, every two hours, with finely chopped pieces of fish or steak.

This terrible regime lasted one long month but her life gradually returned. The tiny crumpled heap became a kitten again. At the middle of the following month she was able to walk. "She was completely cured after five and a half months. She had returned to normal. We had managed to save her and were enormously attached to her. Her parents came to visit her regularly during her suffering and they kindly offered her back to us. We were touched and happy that they had. It would have been very hard for us to be separated from her."

Jessy, a perfect little princess, with a pretty round head, magnificent eyes and pretty paws gloved in white, embarked on her career as a star... and the spoilt child decided to choose her own spouse!

THE STORY OF BALZAC

I met Romy Schneider at a show organised by the Feline Association of France, at Espace Cardin in January 1979. I had come to autograph my book *Les Plus Beaux Chats de France* (The Most Beautiful Cats of France) and I had settled myself a little away from the cages so I would not be in the way of visitors going round. Bent over a page I did not, see Romy arrive. I heard her voice and raised my head. Her hair was drawn back into a bun, her face free from any makeup and she wasn't smiling: "I have come to hide myself here! I hate having my photograph taken when I am not working! It is unbearable to be hounded in this way!" She expressed her concern with deeply moving spontaneity. She responded like a cat before the photographers: she drew in her claws and fled into a corner. She stayed for a while. She flicked through my book and stopped at the page on the sacred cat of Burma: "I would like to have a cat like that! But with all these people and the photographers, I can't go back to see a breeder." She was very particular. She left to make a film with Costa-Gravras and was not able to buy a kitten immediately. I suggested that perhaps a breeder would be able to keep one for her. "I would like to be sure," she said, "that he will be well rounded as the one sold a short while ago." We chatted for a moment about cats and the cinema and then she went off, hugging the walls, with the person who accompanied her, Mme. Das Neves, the governess of her son David.

I realised many years later that every breeder of Birman cats at the feline Association hoped that Romy would choose one of their cats and they waited… As for me, I vowed to think of something else, when one Saturday in February the telephone rang: "Hello, it is Romy! I am calling from Rome. I have read your book. I would absolutely love to have one of Wladimir's kittens!" One of *Wladimir's kittens*? Romy laughed: I knew that if you were listening to me, you would ask what I was talking about!" We had a good laugh together. Wladimir was a beautiful seal point stud cat photographed on a double page of my book. He was the father of my Onyx, then aged six months. Nothing in the world would have made me want to deceive Romy. I liked her. We spoke a little more and exchanged addresses. I gave her the the details of Wladimir de Pouh Miloh's owner Jean-Louis de Pindray. After that we had a couple of postal exchanges and some telephone calls, at terrible moments of her life but I never saw Romy Schneider again. Seven years later. Jean-Louis de Pindray told me what happened.

'Romy telephoned immediately after your telephone conversation. My female cat Uriane de Ligoa, mated with Wladimir was pregnant. Romy said to me "I want a very, very pretty kitten!" I replied that I couldn't be sure to have exactly what she wanted as the kittens were not yet born! She said she would wait. She had an amazing amount of confidence in us'

The order was taken over the telephone and the litter was born on 19th March 1979, there was a small and splendid male kitten. He was a joy! Romy had not seen him, as everything had to be sorted out offer the telephone between Thiais, where the de Pindrays lived and Rome, where Romy was finishing her film *Clair de Femme.* The choice of a first name posed some problems. "I would like to call him Balzac." Said Romy. "That is not possible." The breeder replied. "The name of the kitten has to begin with the letter 'P', as this is the letter for 1979" Romy mocked this: "It is my right not to use the letter of the year!" Finally, the seal point kitten, superb with strong blue eyes was called 'Pere Balzac deRanchipur' At home, certainly he was Balzac for short. When Romy came to collect him he was just over three months old.

Farancine and Jean-Louis remained in contact with Romy Schneider for some time. She adored her cat and wanted to know why he was called 'Ranchipur.' The suffix had been chosen because of the English title *The Rains of Ranchipur* the work by Louis Bromfield an American author. Balzac, a splendid cat very suitable for competitions, only went to one show in his life, at Bordeaux in 1980. The star cat, he enjoyed a regime of favour, in a spacious and comfortable cat cage, in a privileged place but he did not compete. Like Colette, Romy did not like the cages.

Balzac was eight years old on 19th March 1987. He continues to live in Switzerland at the home of Mme. Das Neves.

CHAPTER 7

BREED STANDARDS
AND SHOWING

STANDARD OF THE
SACRED CAT OF BURMA
(FIFE)

Body. Medium-weight slightly elongated, short and strong paws, well proportioned. Rounded feet.

Head.   Good bone structure, full round cheeks, brow slightly convex. Strong chin and average nose, without a "stop". Ears as small as possible, but not too round.

Eyes.   Round or slightly oval, strong blue.

Fur.   Silky texture. Long or mid length depending upon the part of the body: it should be longer on the back and the flank. On the face, short hairs which become gradually longer on the cheeks. Extensive collar.

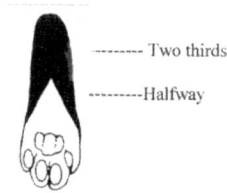

-------- Two thirds

---------Halfway

Colour. The sacred cat of Burma should have the same characteristics as the Siamese on the face ears legs and tail. The rest of the coat should have a very light tint of eggshell colour. The back should be bronzed beige for all varieties. The belly a broken white.

Gloving. The feature of the sacred cat of Burma is its white feet, called "gloves". The white must be absolutely pure. It is possible for the gloves to stop at the beginning of the digits, or to extend as far as the joint between the foot and the leg and no higher. The point must stop between half and two thirds of the distance between the large pad and the back of the heal. Gloves that are slightly higher on the back paws are allowed. Regularity and symmetrical distribution of the gloves is important. The two back paws with one share and the two front paws with the other share or even better all four paws the same.

Tail. Must be of average length and elegant in shape. It is thin at the beginning and thickened at the end.

Comments. This standard presents the usual ideals. Perfect cats are unusual, but defects are more apparent in the Birman, as one irregularity in the gloving is easily seen. It is therefore necessary to select in this breed the cats that show the most regularity, without forgetting the other qualities. What makes the Birman beautiful is the harmony of all the characteristics.

Defects. White marks on dark points incur disqualification. The absence of points on the rear paws, means elimination from the CACIB. The head must neither resemble that of the Persian nor the Siamese.

In the Standard of 1925	
Coat (Length and texture of fur)	20 Points
Colour and markings	20 Points
Head	15 Points
Eyes	15 points
Tail	20 points
Body	10 points
Total	**100 Points**

In the Standard of	1935	1955
Colour and markings	25 points	30 points
Coat	20 points	15 points
Head	15 points	20 points
Eyes	20 points	-
Body	10 points	20 points
Tail	10 points	15 points
Total	**100 Points**	**100 Points**

Standard 1886	
Body	20 points
Head and eyes (shape and colour)	20 points
Colour of Body and Markings	15 points
Gloves on rear paws	5 points
Gloves on front paws	5 points
Points on rear paws	5 points
Regularity	5 points
Tail	10 points
Fur	10 points
Condition	5 points
Total	**100 Points**

THE CERTIFICATES OF THE CHAMPIONS

The cats of a breed presented in a cat show obtain certificates in recognition of their merit, after being examined by the judges. The title of "champion" is accorded to entire cats. The title "premiere" is given to castrated cats. The first stage is the CAC (Certificat d'Apptitude au Championnat Certificate of Aptitude as a Champion). For the criteria on which the cats are judged, see the table "Scale of points" in the "Standard of the sacred cat of Burma". The judge takes notes on a form of the qualities and defects of the cat. For the cat to win awards, he must certainly intend to be presented at a number of cat shows (twenty-one to be the sacred Champion of Europe). Here is the valuation system for the certificates:

- Champion or Premiere: three CAC or CAP and 93 points

- International Champion or Premiere: three CACIB or CAPIB and 95 points

- International Grand Champion or Premiere Six CAGCIB or CAGPIB and 96 points. Obtained in three different countries with three different judges.

- European Champion or Premiere: nine CACE or CAPE and 97 points. Obtained in three different countries with three different judges.

The cats that compete to obtain the title of International Grand Champion or Premiere are classified under the number of their breed and separated according to their sex. Entire cats compete equally for the "Best in Variety" and the "Best in Show" awards. It is understood that castrated cats are able to compete with each other for the "best Neutered" or the "Neutered Best in Show" awards.

A ratified European champion is able to continue to be shown. He receives a prize of honour and is always able to compete for the "Best in Variety" or "Best in Show" awards.

ABBREVIATIONS

CAC — Certificat d'aptitude au Championnat

CACIB — Certificat d'aptitude au Championnat international de Beaute

CAPIB — Certificat d'aptitude au titre de Premior international de Beaute

CAGCIB — Certificat d'aptitude au Grand Championnat international de Beaute

CAGPIB — Certificat d'aptitude au titre de Grand Premior international de Beaute

CACE — Certificat d'aptitude au Championnat d'Europe

CAPE — Certificat d'aptitude au titre de Premior d'Europe.

A BRIEF HISTORY OF CAT SHOWS IN FRANCE

1896. The first cat show was organised in Paris by M. Ferdand Xau and *Le Journal,* a big Parisian newspaper, with the collaboration of M.Porte, the director of the Zoological Gardens. In spite of its success, this show would not become an annual event: there were only one or two in Paris, until 1910

1913. The creation of the **Cat Club of France and Belgium** by Phillippe Jumaud at Saint-Raphael, in the Var region. He organised two cat shows in Nice and Cannes in 1912 and again in 1913.

1914. Two more were organised one in Lyon and one in Aix-les Bains.

1914-18. The French were concerned with other things than cat breeding. The male breeders were called up it was the **First World War.**

1923. Philippe Jumand succeeded in a joint cat and dog show in Cannes on the 19th 20th 21st March 1923." It was a very good idea and would be worth doing again" wrote Francis Marton, a specialist columnist, in *Chasse Peche Elevage*

1924. The idea would be repeated in Cannes, Lille and Marseille

1925.   It was repeated at Angers, Lille and Marseille.

1926.   The first grand international show was organised by the **Cat Club of France and Belgium** on the 14th 15th May at Salle Wagram in Paris. Three hundred cats were presented. The famous Poupee de Madalpour "Burman cat", made his appearance, with two other representatives of the breed. From this date, cat shows became widespread in the large towns in France. Most of the cats presented were Persians or Siamese. They came mainly from France or Belgium, a country that has been interested in luxury cats since the end of the 19th Century. The first Belgian cat show took place in 1891

1927.   The second grand international show by the **Cat Club of France and Belgium** was held in Paris on the 14th 15th January, where the same three Birman cats were presented again. After this there were shows in Strasbourg in April, Charleville in June and so on. A third international show took place on the 27th 28th May in Paris, at Salle Wagram, this time organised by the completely new **Central Feline Society** with the support of **the Cat Cub of France and Belgium.**   There a star was shown: Manou de Madalpour, a Birman bred and owned by Mme Marcelle Adam. In the meantime two new cat clubs were created the **Cat Club of Champagne** and the **Cat Club of Paris.**

1928.   The fourth grand international shows in Paris, on 4th 5th May organised by the **Central Feline Society**

and the **Cat Club of Paris.** Poupee de Madalpour was enthroned as the star.

1929. Two more grand international shows in Paris one on the 8th 9th February by **Cat Club of Paris** and the other on the 24th 26th May by the **Central Feline Society.**

1930. Reims held its first great international show, organised by the **Cat Club of Champagne**.

1931. On the 11th 12th April at the second international show of the **Cat Club of Champagne** in Reims. Reine de Rangoon and Dieu d'Arakan, born 1930, two marvellous cats went of with first prizes.

1932. At the show of the **Cat Club of Paris** on 22nd 23rd January 1932, Dieu d'Arakan was made international champion along with Lon Saito de Madalpour. At the **Cat Club of Champagne** show in Reims on the 2nd 3rd February, the president M. Fournier published, for the first time, the breeder's names and addresses in a catalogue of the show.

1933. The shows continued in France. In Paris, Reims and Amins where the champion Birmans, who had been sold to Belgium, triumphed: Lon Saito de Madalpour, Zaquelle de Mandalay, Djaipour. It was at this time that Pilippe Jumaud (of the cat club of France) broke with the Cat Club of Paris, and would no longer talk to them. 1933 was also the year when Abbot Chamonin organised the First show in Geneva and founded the **Cat Club of Geneva**.

1934. Good news: the three active French clubs decided to pool their experience: the **Cat Club of Paris**, the **Cat Club of Champagne** and the **Central Feline Society** grouped together: the **French Feline Federation** was born. Their books of origins were put together in one maintained by the **Cat Club of Paris.**

1935-39. The shows continued in Paris and the provinces. Another club appeared around 1936 **Les Amis des Chats** but it did not organise any big shows on a regular basis.

1939-45. The Second World War. During this time Mme Ravel, the general secretary of the Cat Club of Paris, tried to keep in contact with the breeders.

1946. In 1946 she organised the first cat show of the post war period: it was a triumph.

1949. Since 1933, at the fourth international cat show in Reims, delegates of foreign clubs had suggested the footings for international accord. In 1949, the **Federation Internationale Feline d'Europe (FIFE)** The (International Feline Federation of Europe) was created, with Mme Ravel as president. It covered eleven countries: Austria Belgium, Denmark, Finland, France, Germany, Holland, Italy, Norway, Sweden and Switzerland.

1952. The Baron of Saint-Palais created another large club: the **Feline Circle of Paris** that would organise cat shows, like the Cat Club, in Paris and in all the large towns in France.

1973. French cat breeding was expanding. Three large clubs were in existence: the **Cat Club of Paris**, (and fourteen clubs in the provinces) **The Feline Circle of Paris** (and nine clubs in the provinces) the **Feline Association of France** (and four clubs in the provinces) The cat shows multiplied. The **Federation Internationale Feline d'Europe** changed its abbreviation to FIFe because its original abbreviation had already been registered - The other entry was in Czechoslovakia - by those in Brazil.

1987. The Federation Internationale Feline d'Europe stuck together and included twenty-one countries, Spain, Hungary, Luxembourg, San Marino, Mexico, Lichtenstien and Singapore, being but a few. What an expansion of the French clubs too about thirty in all the regions which would also become as anarchic as the shows!

In March and June 1987, some "general states" had combined the presidents and secretaries of the principal active clubs, to make a point. There were eleven books of origins. The creation of a large central feline society, similar to the Central Canine Society (which regulated dog breeding under the jurisdiction of the Ministry of Agriculture) would be most welcome.

CHAPTER 8

SIMPLIFIED GENETICS OF THE SACRED CAT OF BURMA

The inspired discovery of Gregor Mendel was to isolate the characteristics which combine themselves in a considerable number to form a particular individual and the inheritance of which is able to be studied over a number of generations. *This discovery of the laws of dominance and recessiveness in genes made in botany can be applied to all species of animals.*

These characteristics (bequeathed by parents when sperm fertilises an egg) are governed by hereditary units called genes, which exist inside billions of living cells, as chromosomes.

Cat cells consist of 38 chromosomes, or 19 pairs of which one pair defines the sex (XX=Female and XY=Male). The sexual cells (Egg and Sperm) take up only 19 chromosomes rather than 19 pairs. At the moment of conception, half the chromosomes are provided by the father and half by the mother, all intermingle. It is inevitably the father who determines the sex of the kittens, as he contributes an X or a Y whilst the mother can only provide X.

The genetic inheritance bequeathed by the parents is called the *genotype.* The visible characteristics are called the *phenotype.* Two cats who appear identical do not necessarily have the same genotype. One of the two may have inherited a gene which does not have a visible effect for the moment but which will reappear after a number of generations.

The genes are called 'alleles' when they find themselves at the same level (the locus) on two chromosomes of the same pair and when they govern the same characteristic. These alleles (or equivalent genes) do not necessarily send the same message to the cell.

A) Homozygote: The message is the same and the two alleles are identical. The kitten is homozygous for this characteristic.

B) Heterozygote: The message is different as each parent has transmitted a different allele. Only one will influence the phenotype: the dominant gene. The kitten is heterozygous but in subsequent generations, the recessive characteristic will become the influencing one if both parents pass on the recessive gene which they possess.

A gene is said to be dominant when its presence on one locus of a pair is enough to influence the phenotype. A gene is said to be recessive when its presence is necessary in the two loci of a pair to express themselves. Dominant genes are written in capital letters and recessive genes in lower case letters.

Most of the important cat genes identified to the present day have been recorded. These relate mainly to colouring, the pattern of the coat and the texture of the fur. The genes responsible for morphology are not known or very little so (see Table). The cat has had mutant colours and long fur for an extremely long time.

When looking at the table, 'the principle cat genes' it is easy to determine the genotype of a Birman male Seal Point. For example Orloff de Kaabaa, the grandfather of our Birmans:

- He did not have a mottled coat, neither did his descendants. The A gene therefore did not exist in his genetic inheritance = aa (single colour fur)

- The colours of his markings (melanin) was black =BB

- Only the extremities were coloured, in accordance with the Siamese Albinism =Cs Cs.

- Orloff, a seal point Birman born of seal points, possessed a pair of dominant genes for dense colour=DD

- He had long fur, genetically inherited from his ascendants=LL(Mutant recessive gene)

- He was male = XY.

- He had white gloves. He therefore had in principle the gene for irregular colouring =SS

- Therefore the genotype for Orloff is able to be written thus: **aa BB cscs DD II XY SS**

The genotype for a blue point is written **aa BB cscs dd II XY SS** The dominant genes DD are replaced by a pair of recessive genes dd (a weak grey pigment).

With regard to the gloving the geneticists are divided. Until recently most believed the Birman cat was homozygous for the dominant S gene responsible for the gloves the appearance of which are always very random. *Roy Robinson an English specialist in feline genetics added to the basic genotype for seal point. He wrote S- i.e with an unknown.*

As for the homozygous condition, the white must be perfect and more widely distributed amongst the coat; however with the Birman the white colouring remains localised on the paws.

There are other theories. Anneliese Hackman, a German breeder, effectively views the gloving characteristic as recessive. Whilst Ken Clarke, an English breeder, believes there is a special gene (g for gloving) responsible for the gloving. Alyse Brisson a young French woman, passionate about genetics, thinks a homozygote or a heterozygote S gene does not act directly on the extent of its expression and that modifying genes exist which curb the expression of the S gene colouring.

Dr Catherine Kreutz, considers, on the basis of notes made during her experiences of breeding, that the sacred cat of Burma is, as far as major genes are concerned, a non white cat (ss). The gloving depends on minor genes and there is an opening through which these genes are able to express themselves. Dr Kreutz emphasises that it is not a question of dominant or recessive genes (except for the major genes which determine a "black and white" or non - white coat. She speaks 'of a continuous genetic variation, a threshold characteristic', which explains why it is difficult to stabilise the amount of gloving in the Birman cat.

The final word is left to Professor Philippe Dreux, who draws this concussion:

'The genetics of the colouring of the cat, which I have studied for a long time, are not as easy for the cat as they are for other mammals. The different theories presented here are directly contradictory and together they show that they are not supported by strict crossbreeding experiences.

In these conditions one cannot say anything particularly plausible which would contribute to a discussion about hypothetical genes of variable expressiveness. Only a strict genetic experiment, making out-crosses with individuals of different colourings, other than Birmans, with the exclusive objective of scientific investigation and an exact description of all the kittens produced, especially those who did not correspond to the standards of the breed, would be able to shed light upon colour determination and thus gloving. It is obvious that Birman breeders would not want to throw themselves into an exercise so contrary to their code of ethics and that geneticists who would be tempted to try, would step back when faced with the cost and constraints of this breed. The ideal situation would be for one side to co-operate with the other, on a basis of mutual understanding and to potentially come up with a solution to this problem.

THE PRINCIPLE CAT GENES

Originating Gene		Mutant Gene	
A	Agouti (light yellow fur ticked with dark patches)	a	Non-Agouti (fur all one colour)
B	Black (melanin-coloured)	b	Brown or chocolate
		b^1	Light brown (Cinnamon)
C	Colouring of the whole coat	c^b	Softened colouring, except on the extremities (Burmese)
		c^s	Siamese markings (only the extremities are coloured)
		c	Albino with red eyes
D	Heavy colouring (normal expression of the colour)	d	Weak colouring (Diluted pigmentation, grey-blue etc.)
i	No inhibition(normal expression of the colour)	I	Inhibition. Absence of yellow pigment (roots of the fur are silver)
L	Short fur	l	Long fur
m	Normal Tail	M	Absence of tail
o	No orange pigment	O	Orange (the pigment is linked with the sex, as it is carried by the X chromosome)
R	Normal coat (straight fur normal length)	r	Cornish Rex (Undulating fur)
R^e	Normal coat (straight fur normal length)	r^e	Devon Rex (Undulating fur without fur on the jaw)
s	Absence of white markings	S	White colouring more or less pronounced
T^+	Tabby (The markings of the wild cat)	T^a	Abyssinian coat (all hairs are mottled)
		t^b	Blotched tabby
w	No white (all the colour genes make an appearance)	W	White is dominant

ADDENDUM

SECRETS OF THE BIRMAN CAT HISTORY REVEALED

Translated and Compiled
by Alwyn Hill

| 1925 | 1926 | 1927 |
| 1935 | 1935 | 1945 |

Introduction to the collection

Having been given permission to publish an English Edition of the book the Secrets of the Sacred Cat of Burma I was always intrigued by the list of publications containing Birman Information. I wondered how many were still available and so began the quest try to obtain

THE SECRETS OF THE SACRED CAT OF BURMA

those I could. The internet these days is a valuable tool for researching all manner of things and so the quest began.

I did research for the Theses written by Jumaud in 1925 and found two copies, one held at Harvard University and the other in the University of Utrecht. Surely there would not be one available elsewhere but with luck I found one in an antiquarian book shop in France. It was in uncut mint condition so unfortunately; to be able to read the content I had to cut open the pages to produce the booklet.

Where possible I have added information on Siamese cats where this breed has been given. Also the Khmer

My thirst grew and I began searching for La Vie a La Campagne 1927 again I struck lucky.

I typed in more searches and came across more books and magazines. Finding Son Altesse des Chats was a real problem because I only had a date and year to go by. It took the purchase of four volumes (48 bound copies of the magazine) of La Campagne before I was able to track this special edition down. However all the volumes are really interesting if anyone is interested in life in the 1920's French interior design, farming methods, cooking, Chateau interiors, Dog and Cat breeds and a lot more besides.

Other books were tracked down eventually from many different sources. Everything was written in French and so began the long process of translation. To ensure they were correct I had them done again professionally by a French linguist.

The copies of the Missions of Auguste Pavie have come from Thailand. The 5 volumes for Gazetteers for Upper Burma 1900 were found on line, as was the India Office List.

I do have many later books about Birmans but these don't reveal any new information and so I think we have here the most precise information there is to be gained in these first few.

Sketches from the VII Paris Cat
Club show at Salle Walgram
Where the Birman was on Display

The Birman description from Dr Phillipe Jumaud Theses 25 March 1925

Like the Siamese this breed, originated in the Far East. Birman cats bred in the temples are heavily guarded and their sale is prohibited. However a few years ago, a pair was acquired by *__M Vanderbilt__ from which came the subjects that were the basis for our observations.

MANNERS
These cats are very sociable, intelligent, happy, loving following their master like a dog. There are however exceptions and one of the subjects observed was particularly savage.

SIZE
These animals have an elongated body, slender legs, well proportioned. The adult weight ranges between 3 and 4 kg.

Chat de Birmanie.

Weight of a Birman (male)

5 days	98 grams
8 days	176

15 days	285
1 month	513
2 months	1122
3 months	1350
5 months	1973
7 months	2775
36 months	3950

HEAD

The head is long with large erect hairy felted ears. The forehead is rounded. Males have a thick tuft of creamy white hair styled oddly in the manner of a griffin. The whiskers are long and wiry. His eyes are an intense royal blue, very mobile.

COAT AND COLOUR

The hair is long, the length of hair half-angora and separated on the back as if by a comb. The tail is very bushy and forms a plume. The colour is creamy white, Siamese but perhaps with more golden tones. The mask, tail, ears, and legs are dark otter and are finished with white gloves stopping below the wrist.

TAIL

This appendage never has nodules; it is long, covered with hair forming a plume, held in the same manner as squirrels.

REPRODUCTION AND BREEDING
Breeding these subjects, we have observed, has been particularly difficult.

***Mme Leotardi** who has had the opportunity to raise multiple litters says she cannot count on raising over one in ten. As for food these animals do very well on boiled fish and cooked salad, others accept raw meat.

SCALE OF POINTS
Here is the scale of points determined for the appreciation of the beauty of these animals.

Coat (length and texture of the hair	20
Colour and markings	20
Head	15
Eyes	15
Tail	20
Body	10
Total	100

Take note of these names as there is more about them in later documents
M. Vanderbilt & *Mme Leotardi*

The Siamese Cat Jumaud Theses 1925

This breed originated in the Far East it occurs in Siam (Thailand), English East Indies (Indonesia) and the Malay Archipelago (Malaysia)

In Europe we are now seeing quite a few specimens which were born in England or France.

Manners: These cats are very intelligent and grooming is easy. About the intelligence of these cats (Jumaud carried out relevant research to prove this.)

The Siamese are particularly sensitive to cold which alters their activity level. During the winter season these animals are in a period of hibernation which though not always apparent is none the less real. This state of hibernation greatly reduces the resistance of young and adult subjects.

(He then notes temperature of in the same cats in summer and winter.)

More than 80% of diseases in Siamese are observed during the winter. Because of this a constant temperature of 20 degrees must be maintained in the cattery, reduced cautiously to 15 degrees for adults. I fear below this temperature fatalities are frequently observed. Sensitivity to cold is the cause of many accidents during transportation by rail and absolutely all unaccompanied travel should be avoided. There are exceptions and that is the Marquise de Scesy Montbeliard whose cattery is located in Haute Marne. She reported a case of a very handsome male age 9 (weighing over 4.5 kg) who spent his nights outside in the snow and 20 degrees of cold.

Siamese cats eat mostly fish and boiled rice but they

are great hunters and devour their game; they are also very fond of sparrows, mice and rats.

Siamese cats have a very extensive voice they use with different intonations, especially around the period before mating.

LE CHAT RACES - ELEVAGE - MALADIES 1926

E LARIEUX & PH JUMAUD

The Birman Cat

Originating, as the Siamese from the Far East the cat of Burma bred in the temples was severely guarded and their sale is prohibited. However a few years ago ***M. Vanderbilt**** was able to acquire a couple whose issue currently exist.

MORALS- These cats are sociable, Intelligent, friendly and caressing in the same way as dogs; there are exceptions and some subjects were particularly wild.

SIZE- These cats have long bodies. The legs are thin and well proportioned. The weight of an adult ranges between 3 to 4 kilos.

HEAD- is long with large erect ears covert in felt like hair; the forehead is bulging. The males have an odd cap of cream white between their eyes in the manner of a griffin. The whiskers are long and wiry. The eyes are intense royal blue, very mobile.

COAT- The hair length is half- angora and separates on the back as if combed. Tail is very bushy and forms a plume.

COLOUR- is that of the Siamese creamy white, perhaps with golden tones. The mask, ears Tail and legs are dark otter. All four legs are terminated by white gloves which stop below the wrist.

TAIL- Never presenting with a nodule; forms a long hairy plume raised and carried like a squirrel.

REPRODUCTION & BREEDING- The breeding of these subjects has always been particularly difficult. The breeder should not count on more than one in ten. For food these animals do very well on boiled fish and cooked salad; others accept only raw meat.

SCALE OF POINTS-

Coat (Length and texture of the hair)	20
Colour and Markings	20
Head	15
Eyes	15
Tail	20
Body	20
Total	100

*Note the name **M. Vanderbilt** again but nothing about an American millionaire*

ALWYN HILL

LA VIE A LA CAMPAGNE 1927
(Article by Dr Phillipe Jumaud)

The cat of Burma is from the Far East. Subjects of this breed, bred in the temples are severely guarded and their sale is prohibited. However a few years ago a couple were imported by ***Mme Thadde Hadish**. (The couple who began the family line de Madalpour) This couple were probably stolen by a servant of the temple, dazzled by promises and who then fled to avoid punishment. Knowing the fanaticism of the Hindus, no one will believe that the priests sold her a couple of their sacred animals, not even for a fabulous price.

Major Sir Russell Gordon part of the British troops charged with protecting Kittahs in 1898 had the opportunity to observe these sacred animals. He drew up a standard that supports our thesis established in 1925.

More the sacred Birman is very sociable, intelligent, happy to be stroked, obedient to commands following his master in the same manner as a dog. He plays with composure, without the presence of his master he becomes nostalgic. He is a quiet animal and lacks the quickness and fire of the Siamese. He seems to be aware of his sacred origin.

Essential Characteristics
Appearance and size: rather small with a long body and slim shapely legs. The sharp claws are strong but

thin and rather brittle. Adult weight ranges between 3 and 4 kg.

HEAD: Is long with erect felt covered ears with white hairs. The forehead is domed the nose is slightly snub. The lower lip is strong giving the impression that the mouth is slightly ajar. The whiskers are long and wiry. Eyebrows are provided, the eyes are a very intense royal blue, sapphire eyes of the legend and deeply melancholy. If the animal is threatened or angry his expression is fierce and reveals that the little beast still intends to be highly independent.

TAIL: The tail is never short, broken, knotted or deviated in any way. At first glance it does not feel like the plume of the Angora. It is not thin it fattens out, one can compare the appearance of the hair to the whip of Setters. The tail is thin at birth but then it thickens. At rest the tail droops slightly and is upturned at the end. When the animal is playing or when he is cross the tail is held at right angles to the body over his back bristling like the huge plume of the squirrel.

COAT: Like Asian cats, the Birman hair is silky and semi long. With a bushy tail that forms a plume like the Angora.

COLOUR: The colour of the mask legs and tail is that of the Siamese, the back perhaps a more bronze tone. When seen in direct sunlight the Birman coat gives the impression of being the colour of burnished gold, hence the name "Golden Cat" the name given by the English who have seen it. Four otter brown legs give the impression of being shod with mittens. It is absolutely necessary for the four white gloved feet to have white until the first phalanx. White peaks rises on the back of the hind legs which gives the impression of short laced boots.

SCALE OF POINTS

Coat:	20 Points
Colour and markings:	20 Points
Head:	15 Points
Eyes:	15 Points
Tail:	20 Points
Body:	10 Points
Total:	100 Points

BREEDING THE CATS:

***Madame Leotardi** observes it has been particularly difficult to breed in her cattery, she had the opportunity to breed ten but claims a Birman male will not breed with Angora cats. **Mme Leotardi** put a beautiful Persian with one of the males. The male flew into a frightful rage and to prevent loss of blood and the poor cat being torn to pieces she covered it with a blanket. Two days later he welcomed and mated a chocolate Siamese.

Offspring from mating Angora cats with Birmans do not resemble the Birman breed. A female belonging to **Mme Leotardi** was accidentally mated by a tabby European short hair produced a completely black, semi long hair female. There is nothing in this litter resembling the mother cat of Burma, not his hair, or colour, or form. Birmans mate easily with Siamese or with the Laotian Lynx cat but the kittens rarely obtain regular gloves. The coat tends to be that of either the Siamese or Laotian.

FOOD: These animals do well on boiled fish and cooked salad. Others will only accept raw meat. They are particularly susceptible to constipation.

To complete this study on the cat of Burma, here are some notes by **Sir Russell Gordon** demonstrating that both Siamese cats and Birmans come from crossing with Annamite cats. "*I think the same as the scientist and explorer **Auguste Pavie** that the Siamese cat is a cross between Birman cats and Annamite cats imported in to the Khmer Empire in the 17 century.*"

The decline of this Empire occurred when closed under the strict action of the Siamese and Annamites. Already in the 7 century "Thai" (Siamese) had invaded the Khmer (Cambodian & Birman) and developed their power at the Khmer's expense. The Khmer were always resistant to the influence of the Indian Brahman. Their closed religion was absolutely top secret from lay people up to the devoted powerful priests and the venerable "Kittahs." These priests were mercilessly hounded and Killed by the

Brahmins in the second Thai invasion in the early 18 Century. Those who could escape fled to the north of Upper Burma, to the impregnable mountains and there founded the underground temple of Lao Tsun. (Home of the gods)

The temple of Lao-Tsun is undoubtedly one of the strange wonders of India, so rare few mortals were asked to contemplate, situated to the east of the lake Incaougji, between Mogaong and Sembo in a semi-desert region with a barrier of impassable walls. In 1898 the last Kittahs still lived there and I was allowed, by special favour, to observe some of their sacred animals. Following the rebellion and during the British occupation based at Bhamo which was very isolated because of its remoteness from Mandalay we had to protect the Kittahs against invasion, looting and massacre by the Brahmin. Their Lama Kittah, the yotagj, received me and presented me with a plate representing the sacred cat, with eyes that are actually two elongated sapphires, at the feet of a strange deity (piece 4108 in my Mildenhall collection) and after granting me the favour to gaze upon the sacred cats numbering one hundred and explained the origin to me.

The legend is pretty but it explains nothing scientifically; It is certain that a race of small yellow eyed Annamite cats, with an elegant and graceful shape and naturally short tail were introduced to Burma around the time of the invasion. Studies related that cat to that of the Isle of man (Cat without a tail) and this animal had been imported to India by English Sailors during the 18ᵗʰ century.

This was observed: Nature has provided that all Asian cats have long fur Angora cats of all colours Persian cats, squirrel cats, Bengalese cats, Chinese dwarf cats on the island of Formosa called "fishing cat" or Japan-cat etc. As it encourages the Arabs and Hindu to protect themselves from the burning sun under large and thick clothes.

Alone among his brethren in Asia the Siamese has short fur. In my opinion I therefore believe with some probability that the longhaired cat of Burma is the ancestor of a Siamese crossed with the Annamite cat without a tail imported by the English. There are still lots of copies amongst Siamese individuals who have yellow eyes and a more or less brindled chocolate coat and whose caudal appendage is reduced to a few centimetres. All Siamese have a break and a knot on the tail when it is long. One can still find indications of the crossing of these two very distinct breeds certainly at the beginning. This assumption is justified and corresponds to the claim emitted by several that the Cat of Burma is due to the crossing of the Siamese cat and the white Angora. It is an unacceptable hypothesis and demonstrably impossible to obtain these results by the mating of Siamese cats and other breeds.

CHATS DE BIRMANIE. 1, 4 et 5. Manou de Madalpour, 1er prix (Paris 1926), à Mme Marcelle Adam. 2 et 3. Poupée de Madalpour, jolie Chatte, 1er prix (Paris 1926), à Mme Léotardi. Les sujets de cette race, au corps allongé, à la tête longue, tirent leur kimo de roi, à la robe garnie de poils longs et soyeux, se distinguent nettement des Chats angoriques, avec lesquels ils ne sympathisent pas. Moins fanfarons que les Siamois, ils sont très sociables, intelligents, gais, mais peu joueurs.

The inscription below the photos state that
Manou de Madalpour won 1 st prize Paris owner Mme
Marcelle Adam
Poupee de Madalpour won 1 st prize Paris 1926 owner
Mme Leotardi

*Notes: The name of the person who obtained the cats has
now changed from*

***M. Vanderbilt** to **Mme Thadde Hadish**. This differs
from the other documents written by Phillip Jumaud. Also
note that **Mme Leotardi** owned Poupee de Madalpour.*

LES RACES DE CHATS 1935

This document is from Jumaud 4 edition Book
(The first edition was published in 1930)

Dr Phillip JUMAUD
President of the Cat Club France

Birman Cat of Burma

ORIGIN: - This breed originated in the Far East. Birman cats bred in the temples are heavily guarded and their sale is prohibited. However a few years ago, a pair were imported by ***Mme Thadde Hadish**** (founders for the family de Madalpour); this couple were probably stolen by a servant of the temple, dazzled by promises and he would have fled for fear of punishment, because who knows the Fanaticism of the Hindus. No one would ever believe that the priests have sold a couple of their sacred animals even for a fabulous price.

In 1898 **Major Sir Russel Gordon** part of the British troops in charge of protecting the Kittahs, had the opportunity to observe these sacred animals. He drew up a standard that corroborates what I established in my doctorate theses in 1925.

MANNERS: - These cats are very sociable, intelligent, friendly and caressing. Like a dog they obey the commands of their master. These cats like to play and play quietly. Without the presence of their masters, they are distant, distant and nostalgic. Animals that are calm who do not have the vivacity and ardour of the Siamese. They seem conscious of their sacred origin.

APPEARANCE& SIZE: - The Birman cat rather small has a longer body, thinner legs but is well proportioned. The claws are sharp, curved but thin and rather friable. The weight varied between three and four kilograms

HEAD: - The head is long with erect ears covered with white hairs. The forehead is slightly domed; the nose slightly snubbed the lower lip large giving the impression of an open mouth. The whiskers are long and wiry.... the eyebrows are provided too. The eyes are moving and a very intense royal blue (the sapphire eyes of the legend) profound and melancholic. If the animal is threatened or angry, his expression is fierce and reveals to all that the little beast still intends to be independent.

COAT: - Like all Asian cats, the Birman cats hair is silky and semi long like an Angora. Those of the tail are less thick than the Angora and form a plume.

TAIL: - The tail never short, broken, knotted or deviated in any direction. At first glance, it does not give the impression of the plume of the Angora; It is thin, not fleshy the hair and appearance can be compared to the "whip" of the Setter. Making of the tail, thinner at birth it becomes wider. At rest the tail is carried drooping, slightly upturned at the end. When the animal is playing or when he is furious the tail is at right angles to the body, carried over the back like a plume of the squirrel bristling and huge.

COLOUR: - The mask, legs and tail are the colour of the Siamese with perhaps more bronze tones on the spine. Seen in direct sunlight the Birman cat coat gives the impression of being made of burnished gold, hence the name "Gold Cat" given to him by the English who were able to see him. Four splendid otter brown legs give the impression of being shod with mittens, gloved fingers of pure white until the first knuckle. At the rear of the hind legs the white goes up to a point giving the impression of short laced boots. The claws are sharp, very curved rather strong but fine and brittle.

SCALE OF POINTS:-
Coat ………………………………… 20
Colour and Markings ………………20
Head ………………………………15
Eyes ………………………………..15

REPRODUCTION AND BREEDING:-

The subjects observed breeding has been particularly difficult. **Mme Leotardi** who had the opportunity to breed several states, do not count to raise more than one in ten.

Birman males do not mate with Angora cats. **Mme Leotardi** presented a superb Persian to one of her

Birman males. He went into terrible rage and had to be covered with a blanket to prevent loss of blood and the poor beast in pieces; whilst two days later making the warmest welcome he mated with a Chocolate Siamese. I never recall products between Angora cats and Birmans. One of **Mme Leotardi's** females accidentally covered by a Tabby Angora produced frightful kittens of which 3 tabby males had short hair, the specimens' absolutely like European cats and one completely black female which had semi long hair. In this litter nothing resembled the mother cat of Burma, not the hair, not the shade, not the form.

The cat of Burma easily mates with the Siamese or Laotian Lynx cat. But the subjects and gloves are rarely obtained. They regularly present the coat and shape of the Siamese or Laotian.

FEEDING:-
These animal do very well on boiled fish and cooked salad, whilst others accept only raw meat. They are particularly prone to constipation.

To complete this study we publish a few notes by **Sir Russel Gordon**, Demonstrating that Siamese originate from the crossing of Annamite cats and cats of Burma.

"Actually, I think and the learned Explorer **Auguste Parve** agrees - The cat of Siam is a cross between Birmans and Annamite cats imports into the Khmer empire in the seventeenth century, when the empire was in decline, rigorously closed by the actions of the Siamese and Annamites.

Already in the 16 century the "Thai's" (Siamese) had invaded the Khmer Empire (Cambodians and Burmese) developing power at their expense. The Khmer were at all times, resistant to the influence of Brahmanic India. Their closed religion was preserved by the almighty priests and the most venerable Kittahs. These priests were mercilessly hounded and killed by the Brahmins in the second Thai invasion at the beginning of the 18 century. Those who could escape fled to Northern Burma to the impregnable mountains and founded the underground temple of Lao-Tsun (home of the gods).

The temple of Lao-Tsun is undoubtedly one of the strange wonders of India few mortals have been known to contemplate. Located east of Lake Incaougji, between Magaoug and Sembo in an area almost deserted, surrounded by a barrier of impassable walls. In 1898 the last Kittahs were still living there and I was allowed the extraordinary favour to observe them somewhat with their sacred animals. Following the rebellion and during the British occupation of the base at Bhamo, very isolated because of its remoteness from Mandalay. We had to protect the Kittah's against Brahmin invasion and we saved them from certain massacre and pillaging. Their Lama-Kittah, Ougji Yotag Rooh greeted me and presented me with a plaque representing the sacred cat at the foot of a strange deity whose eyes were made of two elongated sapphires. (piece 4108 in my Mildenhall collection) and after allowed me the great favour to contemplate the sacred cats numbering a hundred and explained their origin.

The Legend is pretty but does not explain anything about the scientific background.

The fact is certain, that a race of Annimite cats with yellow eyes, slender and elegant shape, small size, a naturally short tail, at one point was introduced to Burma with the invasion. Certain studies communicated to me by **Auguste Parvie** relate this cat to that of the Isle of Man (tailless cat) and that animal had been imported to India by English traders in the eighteenth century.

This is noteworthy:

All Asian cats have thick fur. Angora cats of all colours, Persians, squirrel cats, Bengalese, dwarf cats of Formosa called "Swimming cats" or the Japan-cat etc. Nature has provided this, just as it encourages the Arab and the Hindu to protect themselves from the hot sun under large and thick clothing. Alone amongst his brothers in Asia, the Siamese has sleek fur. I am of the opinion therefore and truly think with some likeliness that the long hair cat of Burma is the ancestor of a Siamese cat crossed with an Annamite tailless cat not imported by the English.

There are still a lot of examples, among the Siamese, individuals having yellow eyes, Fur varying from chocolate to brindle and the caudle appendage reduced to a few centimetres. All Siamese have a break or a nodule on the tail when it is long. One can still find an indication of the juncture of these two very separate races certainly at the beginning.

This assumption is justified and corresponds to advance that emitted by several, pretending that the cat of Burma is the crossing of the Siamese cat and a white Angora. This hypothesis is inadmissible as well as almost constantly demonstrated the impossibility of obtaining these results by mating the Siamese and other breeds of cat. The following item comes from the same book LES RACES DE CHATS 1935

SIAMESE
Dr Phillip JUMAUD

According to explorer **Auguste Pavie**, the Siamese cat is the product of crossing a Birman cat (long hair with an Annamite cat with (no Tail) this cat had been imported into the Khmer empire in the 17 century. It is moreover that some Siamese cats have yellow eyes and where the caudal appendage is reduced to a few centimetres. A break or knot can still be found is the clue to the junction the Birman and Annanmite cat.

ORIGIN: - In Europe there are now quite a few

specimens imported or born in England or France. The first specimens were observed in France in the garden of acclimatisation in 1885 they were given by **M Parvie** who was resident minister for France in Bangkok.

HABITS:- These cats are very intelligent and grooming is easy. They may learn to open doors and cabinets as well as perform acrobatics. They are very attached to their master, they follow him like a little dog, but it is noteworthy that they are thieves and more independent than other domestic cats.

Many Siamese are very sensitive to music and smells. Some scents attract others upset them (Ether Alcohol Mint…) By comparing subjects of the same race , age, weight and even similar conditions we see that in general the brain is much more developed in the Siamese breed deemed by its intelligence.

The Siamese are particularly sensitive to the cold which, in these animals profoundly alters there activity level.

During the winter season these animals are in a period of hibernation which, though not always very apparent is nonetheless real. This state of hibernation greatly reduces the resistance of young and adult cats.

In Siamese more than 80% of diseases are observed during winter, because of this temperament a minimum constant temperature of 20 degrees must be obtained in the breeding livestock. The temperature can be reduced to 15 degrees for adults. Below this temperature I fear fatalities are frequently observed.

This sensitivity to cold is the cause of many accidents during transportation by train and should be absolutely avoided during the winter if the cat is unaccompanied.

One exception belonged to Mme la Marquise de Scey Montbéliard her cattery was situated in Haute-Marne. I can report the case of a very handsome male 9 years old (weight over 4.5 kg) who spent his nights outside in the snow in the cold temperature of 2 degrees.

Siamese eat mostly fish and boiled rice but they are great hunters and devour their game sparrows, mice and they are very fond of rats.

The cat of Siam has a widely applied voice they use with different intonations and modulated especially in the mating period. At this time the cries of the females is reminiscent of beasts.

SIZE AND SHAPE:- They are generally smaller than our cats in Europe. The male is substantially larger than the female. The profile is a bit long but elegant and graceful. The neck and legs are thin.

HEAD:- Always small, wide between the eyes, narrowing between the ears. The forehead if flat and receding, long wide nose. Lips are round and full. Fairly large ears and wide at the base provided with a little fluffy hair inside.

The eyes are almost almond shape slanting towards the nose. The iris is a beautiful blue. The eyes have a reddish hue when the animal is frightened or irritated. The eyes are a crucial point and subject to misinformation such as; the animals were inbred and likely to be anaemic, which makes them look paler, less blue. Cats that have eyes that are blue-green or yellow greenish will be tainted by unexpected defects.

The blue eye colour does not cause a weakening of hearing as in another Breed (*Blue eyed white cats*).

TAIL:- Shorter than the other cats in Europe it is straight and thin like a pointer dog, it is short, curved, broken and even twisted like that of a pig. At the base there is almost always a nodule which is characteristic of the breed.

The issue of the tail of the Siamese has been much written about. And to predict the mode of a long tail has employed fanciful arguments, we will not discuss them because they have no scientific basis. By appropriate selection it is possible to fix the conformation and get only long tails. But it does not prevent the scientific nature of the Siamese breed to always have a knot, break or irregularity of some caudal vertebrae. The opinion of the learned professor Cornevin (which has more weight and value that that of sport breeders or snobs) "examination of subjects born in Siam leaves no doubt on this subject. Of more than 500 subjects imported from Siam I examined only 18 who had long tails and two of the latter category had a breakage at the end." Despite the aforementioned, despite the lack of importance they place on the tail (5 out of 100 points in the scale of points) the English have in their standard states that the tail must be long, steep and slightly raised at the end. Belgians tend to adopt the English mode. In France all tails are admitted in exhibitions and in the scale of points no number was attributed to the tail.

HAIR:- The hair is short, soft and silky to the touch. On the face, legs and tail the coat shines. The coat should be flat revealing firm hard muscles as the Siamese cat should not be too fat.

A long-haired Siamese was exhibited at the Cat Club Newburg by M Harvey, who had brought it back from Malaysia. The parents of the cat were apparently common Siamese who produced Siamese kittens with the exception of the specimen with long hair.

COLOUR:- The colour of the adults are one colour, light cream, pale silver grey, light orange or glossy tan these are the preferred colours and the most popular are the clearest…. On this subject here is a story told by Englishman John Jennings who confirms the favour for subjects with pale coats. "The first cats of Siam which were exhibited in London were light coloured with darker faces and extremities. They came from the palace in Bangkok where it was long believed that the King of Siam maintained catteries for these royal animals at great expense. This was denied by prominent figures and accredited to the Government of Siam. They said that the Royal Siamese cat is a rare variety found in all parts of the country even in Bangkok and surrounding areas. We sometimes find a couple in the palace but there is no official kennel and these cats are looked at as the personal property of the king. This was the case for the old Pekingese Spaniel from old China. Buddhists have a special reverence for the white Siamese or albino animals because it is the preferred form if Buddha returned to earth. Ordinary people do respectful greetings if an animal has a white coat.

The belly and underside of the animal is always pale the back being darker. The head (either whole or in part) the tail, four legs are brown to blackish and blue eyes stand out against the dark mask. The hairs that line the inside of the ears are like white down. Sometimes there is a white spot on the front of the chest between the neck and chest; any sign of a white spot is a sign for disqualification. Collections can be seen in Museum galleries; of subjects with small white spots which mark the ends of the legs in the most bizarre way, around the claws of the middle toe. Whiskers and eyebrows are long very pale hair. Generally there is a blackish spot in the region of the umbilicus it shows very well on a clear coat.

Albinism may occur among the Siamese. Thus a participant CCF M. Fircinai de Cholet recently reported a new case. The observation concerns a young Siamese cat aged 6 months which was all white with pale cream extremities, this cats eyes were red. This small size animal had a knotted tail. Mated many times this cat never re produced.

REPRODUCTION AND BREEDING:- For a long time the number of young born in Europe was very limited because the King of Siam, very jealous of his breeding cats did not export entire males.

The cat of Siam can safely mate other races without extreme danger since Siamese cats are born much smaller than the youth of other races.

Siamese cats come into heat twice a year; spring and autumn sometimes even 3 times in the same year. The heat last for 12 to 15 days often three weeks. It is noteworthy that the female carries about eight days longer than other cats and pregnancy are generally 65 to 66 days.

The cross obtained by mating a Siamese male and common cat in general produces common breeds. In ten observations of this sort once we found a case of the tail produced in the common breed.

At the cat show in Marseilles in 1925 we saw a cat with long hair and the colour of the Siamese breed. The tail was shorthaired and without any nodules.

The number of kittens produced in each litter varies between 2 and 6 and 5 is the most frequent. The average figure represents 38 observations collected by 7 French and Belgian breeders of Siamese cats.

From the age of 4 years the number in each range diminishes and does not exceed 4 on average (personal observations by Mme. Marquise de Saint-Mars)

In the report growth in young Siamese that live on mothers' milk is made rapidly but there are individual differences with the increase of animals placed in the same conditions.

The rapidity of the increase is much lower in young animals that instead of receiving the mothers' milk are subject to a different diet. The same phenomenon was observed in kittens entrusted to cats from other races. In several cases we observed a complete dieback and mortality of 80%.

The young are born white with a small dark line on the edge of the ears. If at the time of birth there is the slightest stain on the pristine coat do not keep them because they are not pure bred. Siamese cats are deemed by a cattery as difficult it is wrong and Mme Marquise de Lingneries who has raised more than ten, tells us that there is no more danger than with other breeds.

FEEDING:- Opinions by breeders are very divided but we want to mention two of them who are particularly qualified because they have raised many very beautiful subjects. Mme Noclain composed meals for her pets, a day of cooked liver (pork veal or beef) cut into small pieces; another day raw minced beef; once a week fish, baked cod or skate alone or with a mixture of bread; another day steak lightly cooked and cut into small pieces.

Mme Noclain has noted that the pale coat persists longer in Siamese cats fed exclusively on fish rather than cats fed with meat. She gives four of five meals a day not offering too much food at once and milk in discretion.

Jennings in his book on cats indicates that food should always be light" everything should be cooked the same, reduced to a jelly" Whether sheep or sheep head or gutted fish all food must be fresh.

THE CLUBS

In France we have a large number of breeders of cats of Siam grouped into Le Club Francais de Chats Siamois (affiliated to CCF) and in England The Siamese Cat Club (affiliated to the National Cat Club).

STANDARD

To conclude this brief study on the cat of Siam below we give the standard scale of points adopted and used by judges.

BODY COLOUR: - The shade of the body must be as pale as possible and preferably cream but the tawny shade is also permitted, without stripes. Spots or marks on the body. The mask, ears, paws, and tail have very clear markings in otter brown. In kittens the mask separated by a fine line and has no stain or defined lines.

The general appearance depends very much upon a good mask that should make the face mostly sable.

EYES:- must be a bright brilliant blue.

HAIR:- is shiny and lying flat in a flat layer on the body.

FORM:- The body must be rather long, legs slim, well proportioned.

HEAD:- is long and pointed.

GENERAL APPEARANCE:- Must retain the following features the curious tail thing striking to the eye. It is important that the subject is not too large, which would undermine the slender type so appreciated. Summarised in each of these peculiarities the cat of Siam must be the opposite of the domestic cat. It is distinguished by a short coat contrasting colours and with a nodule on the tail in particular. Note:- Whilst we admit that cats commonly blue, black, white, tabbies and other colours are cats of Siam the Cat Club of France admits only those who respond exactly to the above Standard.

SCALE OF POINTS

Body colour	20
Size	10
Coat	10
Head	10
Eyes	20
Mask	15
Points report	15
Total	100

Any cat that does not get a minimum of 75 points may not aspire to champion in Cat Club of France.

*Notes- This book establishes without doubt that **Mme Leotardi** did breed Birmans. It also established that Major Gordon was in communication with Auguste Pavie.*

LA VIE A LA CAMPAGNE SON ALTESSE DES CHATS 1935

Baudoin Crevoisier

The cat of Burma sometimes called the Sacred Cat of Burma has been known in France and Europe since 1925. The first example imported into Western Countries would have been to France. Currently, the livestock appears to be in regression, the majority of fine specimens' produced for 10 years are gradually disappearing without always being replaced. This state of affairs justifies a recovery.

ORIGINS. The origins of the cat are discussed, despite its name specifies Burma. Several authors have made an animal of Legend and he would seek the Temple of Lao-Tsun as the origin of these beautiful animals.

Apart from the writings of **Sir Russell Gordon** and **Auguste Pavie** no documents can clarify the origin of these cats. After 6 years of personal research and 10 years breeding in France, the cat of Burma still remains as mysterious as its origin, and no important new evidence could be found and therefore studied.

The first couple of Birman cats brought to France by **Mme. Thadde Hadish**, in about 1925, thus come from the temple of Lao Tsun, where these animals are jealously guarded. The male died on the boat during the voyage, and the female which fortunately had been mated, gave birth to a litter of Birman kittens in Nice. Amongst the kittens a female called Poupee was noticed as having the most perfect Birman type.

The female was then mated by a Siamese cat who at the time had been named Cat of Laos… Because of the lack of a male Birman he had to try a test, partially it succeeds. Litter upon litter and selection on selection, the descendents improved. The preference was given to the youth whose appearance was most like the best breeding stock. Thus was formed the strain *des Madalpour,* named after the first male who perished before reaching France.

Assuming that Poupee had been mated by a Siamese, other breeders crossed Birman cats from the strain Madalpour with gloved Siamese that is to say those who had tips of white on their paws. By frequently renewing the blood of breeding stock, they obtained stronger subjects consistent with earlier type Birmans. It was still another branch of the Birman, much higher than the former that currently appears at the first breeding trials.

It is not impossible that the Birman cat is the ancestor of the Siamese cat, or at least a close relative. There are indeed many similarities between the two races: Type, coat colour, eyes, ease of crossing, habit, and the cry resemblance. The Birman cat could have interbred with tailless cats formally from Indo China that produced Siamese cats whose tail was broken, bent or truncated proves the introduction of blood from the indo Chinese cat. The white paws are sought for Birman cats and are also common in the Siamese cat. Long-haired subjects also appear in litters of Siamese. These phenomena are throwbacks to the ancestors, indicating a common origin between these two races. Finally it should be noted that crossing a Birman and a gloved Siamese gives a high proportion of Birman type in the second generation. Crossing them again gives 80% Birman type kittens.

Principle Champions: Since the beautiful *Poupee de Madalpour* other subjects have been named in this wonderful breed. *Manou, Hiramroi, Lon-Saito, Lon-*

Golden, <u>Ubu</u>, <u>Bijou</u>, Djaipour, Nafaghy, Sitta II, Sita III, Idjadi-Tsun, Yadi. More recent and far superior in beauty and especially hardiness: *Soleil d'Arakan. Bouli d'Arakan, Dieu d'Arakan,* (the most beautiful and most perfect type obtained so far) *Prince de Rangoon, Reine de Rangoon.*

Prototype of Perfection

HEAD: Large and round

NOSE: Rather short

MOUTH: Almost square with long and thick whiskers, lips slightly parted, revealing strong canines.

SKULL: Domed

EYES: Round set a little obliquely, deep blue

EARS: Long and straight, lined with white hairs.

NECK: Strong, and adorned in the male with a thick mane of long hair.

BODY: Long, massive, carried quite low.

CHEST: Broad, back straight.

LEGS: Rather short and broad.

FEET: Finished with long, sharp claws.

TAIL: Long and straight, with no lumpiness or kinks, very bushy, carried often erect over the body.

COAT: The hair is long or medium length according to the part of the body. It is very long and silky around the neck of the male; long on the sides and stomach too, where it is curly. On the tail, the hair is long and flat. The head is covered with relatively short hair which lengthens on the cheeks, like that of the tiger. The fur is slightly wooly on the back of the thighs. The under coat is thick.

COLOUR: The bright parts shade from dark cream to white. (On the belly, below the neck, the ruff and paws). The dark parts are otter brown, as are those of the Siamese. The body has golden highlights, especially when the animal is seen in full light; so the English call it the gold cat. The spine is slightly tanned. The mask is very dark. The legs are slightly lighter and end with the purest white paws. The white colouration on the paws is uneven; between the front and back paws. It also forms a "boot" with the highest amount behind the back paws. The tail colour is darker ending with golden hairs.

WEIGHT: The average is 3 to 4 kg. The male is much heavier than the female.

DEFECTS AND DISQUALIFICATIONS.

HEAD: Too pointed

EYES: Pale blue

HAIR: any colour other than indicated

FEET: Not gloved

TAIL: Bent or too short or too thin

HAIR: short, hard and flat on the body

ABDOMEN AND CHEST: Tinted.

QUALITIES AND ABILITIES.

The cat of Burma is an excellent companion as faithful as a dog can be. He plays very gently, even as an adult. He climbs and jumps like the Siamese, but he is less nervous and fans believe he is more sociable. He is very intelligent and not inferior in any way.

SCALE OF POINTS

Colour and Markings: 25

Coat:	20
Head:	15
Eyes:	20
Body:	10
Tail:	10
Total	100

BREEDING BIRMANS

The breeding of Birmans is easier than any other race of cats The Birman is an indoor cat, but it adapts well to life outside and even seems to prefer this if it is not too chilly. A moderate temperature is sufficient.

His food is nothing special but like all cats he likes meat and it is needed. The meat diet is recommended for Birmans. Never the less he does get used to fish and rice but this food is deficient. Give very little milk to adult Birmans.

Compose the meals in the following manner: Raw meat 3 days per week, fish cooked in water for 2 days, Sardines in oil for 2 days and at the same time mix with the food crumbled stale bread and green vegetables (optional)

For reproduction, the choice of subjects is quite difficult to breed in these rare elements. The male must be almost perfect if the female is not, avoid the opposite as far as possible. In this mating you can very well pass the Siamese and get a Birman with gloved paws. Do not breed before the age of 12 months, especially for young females, that is to say after their first call. The young are like Siamese their breeding is the same; the care and food are identical. After one month wean the kittens, give them milk and rice. Then white fish cooked in water, mix with milk and water, always use cooked fish. Start giving raw meat in small amounts, about a third initially, in one meal, then two to get to 6 meals per week. Only give water to drink.

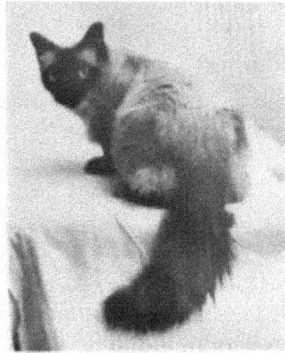

Selection: After the birth of the kittens examine them for notorious defects. Observe the eyes. If they are suffering from a purulent discharge put eye drops in the eyes for two days. If unsuccessful remove the kitten as it could contaminate the entire family. At ten months the kitten takes on the appearance of an adult. The hair begins to grow longer and needs brushing often.

MARKETING: The Birman cat is an aristocratic feline. The cats' beauty is indisputable; its rarity makes it more expensive to acquire. The breeding can be reasonably successful and the success makes you smile. Subjects have achieved great prices. Youngsters sold 2 months after weaning 1,500 to 2,000 francs. Adults vary according to beauty type and perfection. A very good specimen elegant and perfect in all points can be worth 15,000 to 20,000 francs. An average person will pay around 5,000 francs. The prices are fixed in francs and cannot be compared to the price of other like race cats sold for pounds in England. Conversely with respect to prices of Persians sold in England, a Birman would cost some 60,000 francs. This is obviously a lot of money. Interestingly some breeders in Belgium and Italy have acquired the Birman. However France seems to be the only country that currently possesses these rare cats.
BAUDOIN-CREVOISIER.

The Khmer Cat Obtained Recently
JEAN RIEGER

So named because of its Indo Chinese origin the Khmer presents itself as a variety and type very different to the Birman despite a few points of resemblance. There are few representatives of this newly formed race and the only known specimens are currently in France.

ORIGINES: 5 or 6 years ago an old soldier returning from Indo China abandoned a couple of young cats of unknown race with a farmer in the Paris region. These cats grew up and procreated in total freedom, there were many births. Care was little and most perished.

In 1934 I was able to acquire the finest specimens from the male origin. The female had died leaving a daughter to maintain and perpetuate the breed. Now many young females give hope and the future of this race seems assured.

GENERAL APPEARANCE: The Khmer is a good size cat with a strong frame the impression of strength balanced with harmony emphasized by looks and intelligence.

HEAD: Strong Round.

NOSE: Rather short and stout.

MOUTH: Small but powerful.

LIPS: Joined.

WHISKERS: white ticked with brown very well developed attaining a length of 14 cms.

JAWS: With very strong teeth can canines which protrude slightly.

CHEEKS: small.

SKULL: large.

EYES: Round and very slightly diagonal, bright blue, crystal clear and expressive. Appear red in the darkness.

BODY: Long.

WITHERS: normal.

CHEST: Broad.

RIBS: Normal

BACK: Almost straight.

KIDNEY and RUMP: Solid.

LEGS: Strong and muscular. The front ones slightly arched.

FEET: long furred, brown sole, strong sharp claws.

TAIL: Always long and furnished with long hair. Flexible without any breaks or nodules, Carried low with the tip slightly raised.

COAT: Long forming a superb collar around the neck

undulating under its belly. The colour is that of the Birman cream shading to dark otter brown on the head. Legs, feet and the tail have beautiful intermediate tones. The Khmer cat appears to be golden in full sunlight.

The young are born pure white after 3 to 4 days a dark grey undercoat appears which disappears at around 5 or 6 months. The dark undercoat in the young is characteristic of the breed. About 6 months the body is almost white markings are neat and the mask splendid. With age the colour becomes more imprecise because of the dark colour of the hair. (By 18 month the animal is an adult)

Unlike the Birman who must have four legs furnished with white gloves (This obtained by selection) The Khmer must have legs completely brown like the golden otter. Currently a few specimens have white toes, probably because of inbreeding with gloved ancestors. This peculiarity is reserved for the Birman and should be avoided in the future using careful selection.

WEIGHT: a good male should weigh from 4.5kg to 6 kg a Female 3.5kg to 4.5kg

DEFECTS

HEAD: Long

EYES: Too pale or eye disorders

LEGS: Thin

BODY: Insufficient skeletal size or weight

HAIR: Too short.

QUALITIES & ATRIBUTES
The Khmer is a rare beauty, comparable to the Persian for its beautiful fur, The Khmer cat deserves to be appreciated for its remarkable intelligence and mild nature making it a perfect companion.

It adapts well to apartment life. In the countryside it is an intrepid hunter and there is no better ratter. He loves his master and plays but is somewhat noisy. He gets along with all breeds of cat. His voice is quiet with out any wild intonations. He has no defects except those that he is taught.

SCALE of POINTS
HEAD & EYES: 30 points
BODY, LEGS & TAIL: 30 points
COAT & MARKINGS: 20 points
CONDITION: 20 points
TOTAL: 100 points
Principle Champions or candidates
MALES Roi-Pi-You; Prince-Pi- You; Marquis
FEMALES Zezette

MANAGEMENT
Nothing special, however when he is young the Khmer

is sensitive to the cold. Keep the temperature at 15 to 20degrees for the kittens. The room must normally be large bright and airy.

Give a meat diet. Horse meat or beef is just cooked and served warm in small pieces with vegetables.

Select healthy vigorous and good type cats for breeding. Count on around two litters per year. The female carries for 66 days and the little ones average 3 or 4. Give a bit of milk from a month old and then small quantities of cooked fish and meat with vegetables. Serve this completely by the age of 2 months.

I tried crossing my original Male with common cats Persians and Siamese generally the little ones resemble their mother. However a female Siamese of mine from Saigon gave good type Khmers. The only one whose kittens have dark grey undercoats characteristic of the Khmer. Maintenance of cats of this breed is very easy comb and brush every 2 or 3 days. Use the comb from time to time. No special preparation for competition or exhibitions as a cat should be well kept and always ready to face the judge.

MARKETING

At Exhibitions the Khmer has conquered public favour. The price is not above that of a Persian. Surely this breed is going to experience a significant and lasting place since exceptional beauty and softness have joined in the Khmer.

CLUBS & SOCIETIES
There is no special club at the moment but it will be created in a short while.

JEAN RIEGER

Male Khmer Roi Pi- You   Siamese Lolo-Si de
                            Blanc-Mesnil
Jean Rieger bred Khmers and Siamese

NOS AMIS LES CHATS

1947 Marcel Reney
AKA Abbot Chimonin from Switzerland

The Sacred Cat of Burma

Since I saw the wonderful photo of *Dieu d'Arakkan* taken by a reporter at an exhibition in Paris I have been enchanted, Birman cats more than Persians and Siamese exert a peculiar fascination from which we cannot escape. Their eyes are caressing and sweet, the strange beauty of their fur, their most endearing character making friends differently from all other cats.

Also after 15 years I have not discovered anything enlightening about the mystery of their origins.

In 1926 Ph Jumaud wrote in **Les Chat** *"Originating in the far-east, like the Siamese, Birman cats bred in the temples are heavily guarded and their sale is prohibited but some years ago M. Vanderbilt was able to acquire a couple coming from subjects that currently exist."* Since then various journal articles and books will add to this short story. Jumaud himself dedicated nearly six pages to the Birman in the 1930 edition of his other work "**Les Races de Chats. In Minerva** Dr Fernand Mery published the legend of Sinh the ancestor of the cats from the temple of Lao-Tsun. M Boudoin Crevoisier especially has multiplied his articles**, Revue Feline Belge** in 1931**, Jardins et Basses-Cours** in 1932, la **Revue Feline de France** in 1933 and **Chasse Peche Elevage** in 1935

I have read all these documents without being able to shed more light on the origin of this wonderful breed. I have tried the livestock from M. Baudoin-Crevoisier and now sketch the picture of what we know. But my honourable reader be warned the thirst for the unknown will not be further enhanced.

So ***American Millionaire M Vanderbilt** during a cruise in the Far-East manages to obtain, for a gold reward, a couple of sacred cats. Undoubtedly these were stolen from the Temple of Lao-Tsun by an unfaithful servant. This couple were given to **Mme Thadde-Hadisch**. However the male died accidentally on the boat and the female Sita went on to produce a nice litter of kittens with one perfect one Poupee.

Baudoin said in an article in 1933 "Poupee can not be mated to a male of the same race. The cat used was a Lynx of Laos belonging to a doctor in Nice a cat resembling a Siamese with very blue eyes. The young being Birman and Laos crosses" By successive crosses the perfect Manou de Madalpour was born, very similar to his mother Poupee."

More information from Baudoin writing in 1935 "The female was then mated to a male Siamese who for the occasion had been named cat of Laos….." It was that in 1933 wanting to get to the bottom of this bizarre story I wrote to the famous doctor in Nice M. Prat. He replied "Actually we had several Siamese including *Youyou* But we know nothing of its origin….. I know nothing about a Mme. Hadisch **Vienna**. *(Note The home of Mme Thadde Hadisch was probably **Vienne** in France)*

I demanded more from M. Guy Cheminaud a great hunter who had lived in Laos. His books are familiar to fans of stories of deer hunts. What he thought of "the lynx cat of Laos" His reply was there are no cats in Laos as a species distinct from the Siamese cat.

Unsupported history built by Jumaud & Baudoin collapsed then as the principle witness knew nothing of owner of the legendry "Cat of Laos" Mme Thadde Hadisch or the lynx cat.

There was also in their tale about **Mme Leotardi** a great adventurer who, it seems, had possessed the Birmans from Mme Hadisch. Manou de Madalpour in his last days surrounded Mme Marcelle Adam with his affection. She certified to me in Paris that Mme. Leotardi, before disappearing mysteriously, told the story of the Burman as Jumaud and Baudoin wrote it.

In 1933 I published an article in Chasse Peche Elevage for new information; Baudoin took account of it in what he wrote for Son Altesse Le Chat in 1935. In there he declares "Apart from the writings of Sir Russel Gordon and Auguste Pavie no documents can clarify the origin of these cats. After six years of personal research and ten years of breeding in France, the Birman is still as mysterious as its origin and no important new specimens could be seen and consequently studied"

What intrigues me the most, set out in this case is,

it relies on the testimony by Jumaud and Baudoin to give an impression of the truth to the story of the Birman, Jumaud wrote of an English major Sir Russel Gordon "Major Russel Gordon part of the British troops charged with protecting the Kittahs in 1898 had the opportunity to observe these scared animals." Read a note on the temple of Lao Tsun, Built in the early 18 the century by khmer priests, kittah's whose religion was very secret and completely closed to low and lay people. He cites Russel Gordon himself:

"The temple of Lao- Tsun is undoubtedly one of the strange wonders of India and few people have ever gazed at it, in an almost deserted area surrounded by barriers of insurmountable walls. Still living in 1898 the last Kittahs allowed me to observe some of their sacred animals. As a result of the rebellion and during the English occupation of the base at Bhamo, the base very isolated because of its remoteness from Mandalay. We protected the Kittahs from a Brahmin invasion and we saved them from certain massacre and pillage. Their Lama Kittah Yotag Rooh-Ougji received me and gave me this plate representing the cat at the feet of a weird sacred Deity whose eyes were made of two elongated sapphires and after the badge allowed me to contemplate the cats numbering one hundred and explained the origin"

I lobbied to get a photo of the piece mentioned by Sir Russel Gordon and an accurate indication of the magazine or book or text that has been published this was in vain.

I tried, in vain, to find new details on the existence of Mme Thadde Hadish and Mme Leotardi.

Also the origin of the Birman remains shrouded by an impenetrable veil to punish those who had desecrated by their sacrilegious theft the temple of Lao-Tsun. The rest Baudoin after trying breeding Birmans and asserting that this was easy, he surrendered in 1935. The date on which he sold to Princesse Ratibor Hohenlohe, for the price of 300,000 French francs a splendid male, who had won the votes of all the public in France and abroad *Dieu d'Arakhan* and some five or six remaining males and females.

In Switzerland and Belgium amateurs who attached themselves to these cats without parents and have saved the race. In France two or three breeders still have half-Birmans at the beginning of 1940. As for the cats owned by Princess Ratibor they had some strange adventures. Bequeathed by the princess to S.A.R. the duke of Aosta, they were hidden for a while. It was a cousin of the latter the countess Giriodi Panissera who finally manages to gain possession of the cats.

In Autumn 1936 I had the honour, whilst visiting the castle Francavilla Bisio, near Nova Ligure, to see closely the results obtained through the kindness and patience of Lady of the manor. Besides **Dieu d'Arakhan** and **Reine de Rangoon** there were seventeen cats and fourteen kittens some showing much promise. What happened to this wonderful collection of cats I happily call "The most beautiful cats in the world"

Since 1940 I have not heard from Francavilla and all I have to console me is the nostalgic memory of the great court of the chateau in which my dear friends with white paws frolicked in the light with the gentle Lady of the manor....

To better enjoy these fabulous animals I want to quote the legend told to Russel Gordon by Yotag Rooh-Ougji. Dr Fernand Mery, who has published in *Minerva*, She says it was said "One summer evening, near the Spanish border, by a blonde animal lover....."

"Our friend began gently. In this time, in a temple built on the slopes of Mount Lugh, lived in prayers the very venerable Kittah Mun Ha, great lama precious among the precious, the one whose god Song Hio had a beard of gold braid...

"Not a minute, not a glance, not a thought, his existence was devoted to worship, contemplation and pious service of Tsun Kyankze the goddess with Sapphire eyes, the one who presides over the transmutation of souls, the one that allows kittah's to relive in a sacred animal for the duration of his animal existence, after his animal existence to take the body and halo of total perfection of holy high priests. With his dear Oracle meditated Sinh an all white cat whose eyes were yellow, yellow to reflect the golden beard of his master and the golden body of the goddess the eyes of heaven… Sinh, the cat adviser, whose ears, nose, tail and extremities were the dark colour of soil, the mark of defilement and impurity that affects or may affect the earth.

One evening, the malevolent moon had permitted, the cursed Phoums, Siam abhors, coming and approaching the sacred enclosure. The high priest Mun Ha, without ceasing to implore the cruel destinies, went gently into death, in front of God and the despair of all his overwhelmed Kittahs, with his cat at his side.

That's when the miracle happened… The miracle of an instant transmutation: I one bound Sinh was on the throne of gold. And perched on the sagging head of his master… He braced himself on this face loaded with years and which for the first time, no longer looked at the goddess … remained and in turn froze before the eternal statue, one saw the bristly hair of his white spine suddenly become yellow gold and his eyes became blue, vast and deep as the eyes of the goddess. As he turned his head slowly towards the south gate his four paws, which had touched the venerable skull, became a dazzling white, until covered by the sacred silk clothes. As he turned his eyes away from the south gate the Kittah's obedient to the requirement of this loaded hard glance, rushed to close the heavy bronze doors on the first invader…

The temple was saved from desecration and looting… on the seventh day Sinh had not yet left the throne, then without making a movement and eye to eye with the goddess he died. Priestly and mysterious carrying the soul of Mun Ha, too perfect henceforth for the earth, to Tsun Kiankze … When seven days later the priests assembled before the statue to decide upon the successor to Mun Ha they saw all the cats in the temple running…. And all were dressed in gold and with white gloves. All their yellow eyes had all changed to deep sapphire blue. They all silently surrounded the youngest of the kittahs and thus he was chosen by the will of the goddess and the reincarnated ancestors.

Now, says the story teller, a cat that died in the sacred temple of Lao Tsun is the soul of a kittah who has never resumed his place in paradise with Song Hio, the god of gold. Woe she says to anyone who hastens the end of one of these wonderful beasts even if he did not mean to. He will suffer the cruellest torments until he has soothed the troubled spirit that was disturbed.

Sir Russell Gordon already remarked the legend is pretty but it does not explain anything of scientific origin. It will remain a mystery for a long time. Some authors have said that Birman were due to crossing a Siamese with a white Persian. Russell Gordon compared his observations with those communicated by Auguste Parvie. Who wrote to the contrary: "My opinion is to believe with some probability that the longhaired cat of Burma is the ancestor of Siamese crossed with an Annamite cat without a tail imported by the English."

This opinion sheds no light behind the Sacred cat of Burma since they forgot to say what this Annamite cat was and it obscures the Siamese cat a bit more, as discussed in the next chapter.

Jumaud gave a description of the Birman in accordance with the standard published by Russell Gordon. This description is partly correct: I have carefully studied the Birman in France, Switzerland and those at Francavilla. I have published a few points here that differ.

Photos of the Birman give an approximate idea of the extraordinary beauty of these cats. They do not tell the exquisite character of these charming and mysterious beings. Anyone who had the rare pleasure of owning one in their home said to me: Once we have experienced the sweetness and intelligence of the Birman we can study at leisure the unfathomable mystery in their eyes like a deep dark sea, we always dream of having one near not only Mme. Giriodi the countess, who was surrounded by a courtyard of these valuable animals. Mme. Marcelle Adam who was the devoted "mother" of Manou de Madalpour would contradict me... Also I caress the secret hope of one day finding a couple that will remind me of the hugs and joy which Sinh, **Poupee de Mandalay*** *(Note not to be confused with Poupee de Madalpour)*, Kebir, Fatima and Fakir One showered on me... Sweet Fatima who died pining after the sudden death of Fakir.

But why do you call these cats sacred cat of Burma you ask, because of the legend assigns them to this fabulous home on the one hand. Secondly, to distinguish it from a variety of Siamese cat that exists in the US. A Siamese cat with yellow eyes and a chocolate coat, that the Americans have baptised Burmese cats. Burmese cats are cats with short hair, which is given in the description below. Whilst the Sacred Cats of Burma are longhaired cats with blue eyes and white gloved paws.

Standard and scale of points

Birman cats are very sociable, intelligent, lively, loving; obey the commands of their masters in the same manner as dogs. They play a little or quietly. Without the presence of their masters they become lonely. They are apartment animals without the liveliness and spirit of the Siamese; they seem to be aware of their sacred origin.

APPEARANCE:
The body is long and solid carried low on short, strong legs. The claws are long.sharp and fragile. The size is intermediate between that of the Siamese and the Blue Persian.

HEAD:
Big and strong, massive even and round, like the Persian and not like the Siamese who's is thin and elongated. The nose is short and snub, the forehead is slightly rounded. Well developed cheeks and mouth ajar. The whiskers are long. Eyes a little oblique are an intense blue (sapphire blue of the legend) with well furnished eyebrows.

FUR:
The fur is long to mid length, depending on the part of the body. It is very long on the back and sides with an abundant collar. The texture is silky, except on the belly where the hair is wavy and a bit woolly. On the face the hair is short, but becomes longer on the cheeks. The tail when the cat is old enough it presents as a plum; thin at birth it becomes very thick. At rest it hangs but then it is reversed and carried over the back like the squirrel when the animal is playing or is angry.

COLOUR:
The Birman has the same trademark characteristics as the Siamese, on the face, ears, legs and tail: They are scorch brown but with golden high lights. The rest of the body is a very light cream colour. In addition, it has white gloved paws; absolutely white up the first toes on the forepaws, whilst higher and rising to a peak on the back of the hind feet. These white markings, respond to the legend of Sinh and are essential in the standard for the Birman.

TAIL:
The tail is fairly long, straight no breaks or nodules. It is covered with very long, silky hair which lies flat not puffed out like a Persian.

The Scale of Points

Colour and gloving	30
Head	15
Eyes	15
Tail	15
Body	10
Fur and condition	15
Total	100

BHAMO AND DISTRICT

The above map is the part of upper Burma where the Birman is said to originate from. From the map you can draw an imaginary triangle between Indawgyi Lake, Mogaung along the Irrawaddy River to Sinbo and down to Bhamo in the south. In 1900 a series of Gazetteers describing the people, culture, towns and villages and terrain of upper Burma were produced. From these gazetteers one can read that there was a military peacekeeping settlement in Bhamo at the time major Gordon was there. One can also read about the Burmese culture to tell stories similar to the one our Birman Legend is based on part truth part fable. It was true that there were marauders who would go round looting and pillaging and that the military were responsible for acting to arrest these people. Having read this could it be that the temple of Lao Tsun was a real place too. Checking through the many village names I came to one called Kamiang Here is what was written.

Kamaing;- A village on the Mogaung chaung some 30 miles above Mogaung, is the headquarters of the Kamaing township, Mogaung subdivision of Myitkyina district. The surrounding country is deeply flooded in the rains and there is very little land suitable for an extension of the village, though plenty available for cultivation. Most inhabitants are connected with the India rubber trade either as middlemen between the Kachins and Chinese or as boatmen to convey the india rubber from Sadusut or Laban higher up the river, to Mogaung.

Wondering if Lao Tsun could be an actual village name I found the following.

Law Sun;- A village on the Namten *chaung in the Mogaung subdivision of Myitkyina district t has 61 houses and two hundred and forty buffalo There is a small *pôngye *kyaung. A few guavas and custard apples are grown. It is said to have been founded about 1830 by emigrants from Kamaing, (written Kar Maing on Google map) who left because the land was inundated. Le and taungya cultivation are practiced.

* chaung = Stream

* pôngye = Monk

kyaung = *Temple*

The land in the area behind the stream is very mountainous so was this the original home of our Sacred cat of Burma. We have seen many different spelling errors for place names in other literature so is Law Sun the correct spelling for the temple of Lao Tsun. The area is correct the fact the military were protecting the area is correct.......read on about Major Gordon.

MAJOR GORDON

Major Sir Russell Gordon has remained a mystery for a very long time. However now the following the information has been unearthed from the Indian Army List 1905 and more may be about to change this.

There was no record for a Major Sir Russell Gordon ever being in the Army and no mention of a Sir Russell Gordon either. However, there is a record for a Major Ramsay Frederick Clayton Gordon serving in Bhamo at the right time.

Here is what is known about Ramsay Frederick Clayton Gordon

He was born in Middlesex in 1864 and had a glittering military career.

Record details

Name:	Ramsay Frederick Clayton GORDON
Event type:	Biography
Start date:	
Start year:	1864
End date:	
End year:	1943
Biographical notes:	Lt-Col, Indian Army; Who was Who IV p.448
Transcribed by:	British Library
India Office Records Reference:	
Source name:	Who was Who IV p.448
Source year:	
Source edition:	
Presidency:	

He appears here in the 1881 Census age 16 at Wellington College Sandhurst Berks

He joined the Indian army as a Major, Commandant military Police in Burma. His first command in Burma was 23rd August 1884 then after military service as deputy inspector General of Military Police from April 1901 to April 1902 and again as commandant of Military Police from November 1902 as noted from the Indian Army Records List.

GORDON, RAMSAY FREDERICK CLAYTON, Major, Indian Army (commdt., mil. police, Burma).—First commn., 23rd Aug., 1884 ; after mil. service acted as dep. inspr. gen. of mil. police, Burma, from April, 1901, to April, 1902, and again from Nov., 1902, with subs. appt. of commdt. of mil. police.

Rearching on the family history site Ancestry.co.uk a record came to light. it was a small notice of Major Gordons death in the Times newspaper. He had died at his home in Cheletenham. I contacted our local History Society and learned that his obituary was published in the Cheltenham Chronicle and we managed to get a copy from the Library in Cheltenham.

By some strange coincidences at the time I was searching on Ancestry Ramsay Gordon's grandson was also doing research and we made contact.

DEATH OF LT.-COL. R. F. C. GORDON

The death has occurred at his residence, Bibury, Montpellier-drive, Cheltenham, of Lieut.-Col. Ramsay Frederick Clayton Gordon, C.I.E., late 15th Lancers (Cureton's Multanis) at the age of 78 years.

Educated at Wellington College, he adopted a military career and spent most of his life in India and Burma, and was at one time Inspector-General of the Military Police. For several years he was Private Secretary to Sir John Hewett, Governor of the Punjab.

LIEUTENANT-COLONEL IN 1910

Commissioned a lieutenant in the 18th Hussars in 1884, he was promoted captain in the Indian Service Corps in 1895. In 1902 he was a major in the Indian Army and was promoted to lieutenant-colonel in 1910, serving with the 15th Bengal Lancers (Cureton's Multanis). He held the Legion d'Honneur.

On his retirement in 1920 Lieut. - Colonel Ramsay Gordon settled in Cheltenham. Ill-health prevented him from taking an active part in public life.

He underwent a serious operation in January of this year and did not recover.

It was from his grandson I learned that the family did own some Siamese cats although the grandsons own father didn't recall if it was his father who was most interested in the cats.

The grandson had done research trying to find out what the Legion d'Honneur was for. Although listed the records were not available so had probably destroyed during the Second World War.

I learned that the family used to spend part of the year in France only a few kilometers away from Auguste Pavie's home town Dinan Brittany.

With all these clues it is very possible that Phillip Jumaud, Auguste Pavie and Major Ramsay Gordon did eventually become friendsin France and the name Russell was a lapse in memory written by Jumaud in those very early documents about the Birman. When Ramsay would still have been serving in the army.

So far the grandson has not managed to find the plaque of the deity with sapphires for eyes. His father did tell him that military men travelled light..... Also some other member of the family may have inherited the plaque, so at the present time this has not been found.

AUGUSTE JEAN-MARIE PARVIE

|

Born in **Dinan** 31 May 1847 Auguste Pavie was a
French colonial civil servant, explorer and diplomat
who was instrumental in establishing French control
over Laos in the last two decades of the 19th century.
After a long career travelling, producing maps and
documenting the terrain on his travels in Cambodia
and Cochin china up to border with northern Burma,
he produced the a number of manuscripts including
maps called The Missions de Pavie. He became the first
French vice-consul in Luang HYPERLINK "http://
en.wikipedia.org/wiki/Luang_Prabang"HYPERLINK
"http://en.wikipedia.org/wiki/Luang_Prabang"
HYPERLINK "http://en.wikipedia.org/wiki/Luang_
Prabang" HYPERLINK "http://en.wikipedia.org/wiki/
Luang_Prabang"HYPERLINK "http://en.wikipedia.
org/wiki/Luang_Prabang" HYPERLINK "http://
en.wikipedia.org/wiki/Luang_Prabang"Prabang in
1885, eventually becoming the first Governor-General
and plenipotentiary minister of the newly formed French
colony of Laos.

His missions never reached Bhamo and the breed he was
familiar with was the Siamese kept in the Royal Palaces.
It was the practice for the king to present a pair of Royal
Siamese to people who had been in his service and so it

was that Pavie did bring two to France as documented in Siamese section of Les Races du Chats 1935.

He died on 7 May 1925. and there is a monument in his honour in the gardens in Thourie France.

MADAM LEOTARDI

Mme Leotardi is known to have shown Poupee at the Cat Club Paris show as the text for the picture below shows, where it says Poupee won first prize. Also at the show was Manou (Mispelt Manon) de Madalpour owned by Mme Marcelle Adam.

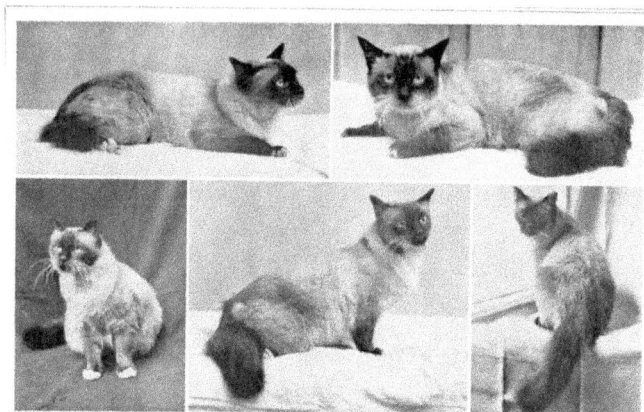

CHATS DE BIRMANIE, 3, 4 et 5. Manou de Madalpour, 1er prix Paris 1924; a Mme Marcelle Adam, 1 et 6. Poupée de Madalpour jolie Chatte, 1er prix Paris 1924; a Mme Leotardi. Les sujets de cette race, au corps allongé, à la tête longue, aux yeux bleu de roi, à la robe queue de souris beige et argenté, se distinguent nettement des Chats asiatiques, avec lesquels ils ne signalent pas. Moins joueurs que les Siamois, ils sont très paisibles, intelligents, gais, mais peu voyeurs.

Here is a second report about Mme Leotardi wining prizes at a show June 1925 Unfortunately this paper doesn't name her cats.

**Archives départementales du Maine-et-Loire
Presse**
Le Petit Courrier - Juin 1925

Le Concours des Chats

PALMARES

Siamois neutre

300. M. H. — Mme Tomery.

Siamois clairs (mâles)

301. 1. Prix. — Mlle Hallouin.
311. 2. Prix. — M. Renaud.
306. 3. Prix. — Mlle Louveau.
307. M. T. H. — Dr. Thouvenin.
305. M. H. — Mlle Louveau.
308. M. H. — Mme Boulard.

Siamois chocolat (mâles)

304. 1. Prix. — Mlle Dandlœuf.
309. 2. Prix. — Mme Bachelier.

Siamois claires (femelles)

312. 2. Prix. — M. Renaud.
313. 3. Prix. — Mlle Pons.

Siamois chocolat (femelles)

310. M. H. — Mme Bachelier.
314. M. H. — M. Rouxel.

Siamois (jeunes)

310 bis. 2. Prix. — Mme Bachelier.
312 bis. 2. Prix. — M. Renaud.
315 bis. 2. Prix. — Mme de Louplac.

Chat de Birmanie (femelle)

317. 1. Prix. — Mme Léotardi.

Chat de Birmanie (jeune)

317. 3. Prix. — Mme Léotardi.

Chat de Perse blanc (mâle)

318. 1. Prix. — Mme Brassart (certificat de championnat).

Chats de Perse blancs (femelles)

321. 1. Prix. — Mme Brassart.
319. 2. Prix d'élevage. — Dr Bonvallet.

Chats de Perse (classe de couples)

318-321. 1. Prix. — Mme Brassart.

Chat de Perse bleu (mâle)

322. 1. Prix. — Mme Brassart.

Chat de Perse bleu (femelle)

324. 1. Prix. — Mme Brassart (certificat de championnat).

Chats de Perse noirs (mâles)

320. 1. Prix. — Mme Brassart.
323. 3. Prix. — M. Citeau.

From these two documents it is clearp that Mme Leotardi did own Poupee and was showing in France. She also registered her cats in the French Livre d'Origine. There is a place called Vienne just 30 miles from Lyon and it would seem logical that Mme Leotardi was a French lady and Vienne was her home rather than Vienna in Austria.

AUTHORS COMMENT

I finish the Birman History at this point because any later books only have the writtings of Jaumod and Crevosier as written in the original sources.

CLUBS FOR THE BIRMAN
AROUND THE WORLD

Denmark:

Birmaringen
Website: www.birmaringen.dk
Klubben For Den Hellige Birma
Website: www.birma.dk

Australia:

The Birman Cat Club of Canberra Inc.

Website: www.geocities.com/Petsburgh/3039/defaultpage

Birman Cat Fanciers of Queensland
Website: www.birmanclubqld.com

The Birman Society Inc.
http://www.thebirmansociety.com

Sacred cat of Burma Fanciers Association of Australia Inc.
http://www.hotkey.net.au/~birmancats/index.htm

Birman Cat Club of Australasia Inc.
http://www.birman.asn.au HYPERLINK "http://www.birman.asn.au/" HYPERLINK "http://www.birman.asn.au/" HYPERLINK "http://www.birman.asn.au/"/

United Kingdom:

The Birman Cat Club
Website: www.birmancatclub.co.uk

The Northern Birman Cat Club
Website: **www.northernbirmancatclub.co.uk**

The Seal and Blue Point Birman Cat Club
Website: www.birmancatuk.co.uk

Sweden:

The Midnight Sun Society for the Sacred Birman Cat
Website: www.birma.eu

Switzerland :

Le Club Suisse du Sacré de Birmanie
Website: www.birmaclub.ch/

New Zealand:

Birman Cat Club of New Zealand Inc.
Website www.geocities.com/birmancatclubofnz

America:

Sacred Cat of Burma Fanciers
Website: http://www.scbf.com.

National Birman Fanciers
Website: http://www.nationalbirmanfanciers.com/

France:

Cercle du Chat Sacre de Birmanie
Website: www.cerclechatsacre.org

Holland:

Dutch Birman Cat Club
Website: www.felikat-heiligebirmanen.nl

Norway:

Norske Birmavenner
Website: http://home.c2i.net/birmavenner/

South Africa:

Sacred Birman Fanciers Group of Southern Africa
Website: Http://sbfgsa.tripod.com

Germany:

Birma Club Deutschland
Website: birma-club.de

Italy:

Italian Birman Club
Website: www.agabi.net

APPENDICES

BIBLIOGRAPHY

Birmanie	Gabriel Le Ramier. Guide Arthaud
Chasse Peche Elevage	Monthly magazine 1924-34
The Cat A breeder's handbook	Marguerite Ravel Publisher: Crepin-Lebond
What colour will my kittens be?	Alyse Brisson
The Cat Book	Michael Wright, Sally Walters Publisher; Septimus
Minerva	Weekly magazine 1925-38
Our Cat Friends	Marcel Reney Publisher Charles Grasset, Geneva 1947
Cat Breeds	Veterinary thesis of Philippe Jumanud 1925 Published in 'Tablettes' at Saint-Raphael
Trends in Genetics	Cat Genetics, Roy Robinson. Publisher: Elsevier, Cambridge
Vie A La Campagne	Monthy magazine puplisher Hachette

ACKNOWLEDGEMENTS

FRENCH EDITION

We would like to thank all the people who kindly allowed us access to their documents or gave us important information...

...On Burma:
Mlle Catherine Champion
M. Guy Lubeigt, Researcher at CNRS, in charge of Burma mission.

...On the Birman cat in Italy and Switzerland:
M. Piero Andreini
Mme Gabrielle Bernardi
Mme Franca Gabriele, the president of the club The Sacred Cat of Burma at Turin
M.J. Mannes an international judge of FIFe.

...On genetics and primitive origins:
Dr Giorgio Bernardi, biologist at CNRS

Prof. Bernard Conde zoologist Zoological Museum Nancy

Prof Philippe Dreux, professor of zoology at the University of Pierre and Marie Curie

Veterinary Doctor Jean-Louis Guenet, geneticist at the Pasteur Institute

Veterinary Doctor Catherine Kreutz, breeder of sacred cats of Burma.

Prof. Jacques Nouvel, president of the Cat Club of Paris and the French provinces.

...On breeding the sacred cat of Burma:

Mme Francine Chauvelon de Pindray and M.Jean-Louis Chauvelon de Pindray, International judge of FIFe.

Mme Renee Pottrain, president of the Cat Club of Northern France

Mme Madeleine Vandalle, friend of Mlle Boyer.

Also thanks to Mme Suzanne Arelli, the general secretary of the Cat Club of Paris and Mrs Elizabeth Grison, librarian at the National Veterinary School at Maisons-Alfort and to M. Georges Lanthoinetter, archivist at Editions Hachette, for the documents which he trusted us with or allowed us to photocopy. Finally, thanks to Mme Dominique Patte for her assistance in tracing the foreign newsletters.

ACKNOWLEDGEMENTS

ENGLISH EDITION

Thank you to the original publisher Bornemann Edition in Paris for releasing the copyright to allow this English edition to be printed.

Thank you to Michelle Hill for all her hard work in translating the original book.

To Mrs Vivian Creasy-Smith for giving me permission to use photographs from her book The Birman Cat World Wide.

To the Sacred Cat of Burma Fanciers in America for allowing me to use photographs held in their archives.

LIST OF ILLUSTRATIONS

ALWYN HILL

www.ingramcontent.com/pod-product-compliance
Lightning Source LLC
Chambersburg PA
CBHW052110030426

42335CB00025B/2916